Introduction

Monday 23rd of March 2020 a day we'll all remember, the day life changed when lockdown commenced. I'll remember this day for the rest of my life, as having suffered from depression for over thirty years, and less than a year since I came within seconds of ending my own life. I found myself trapped alone in my childhood home, where for five years in the eighties, I suffered horrific abuse at the hands of an officer from the local Sea Cadets, who'd befriended my family. This was the cause of my depression in the first place. But luckily for me, instead of taking my own life last May, as a tribute to my late book loving Mother, I decided to try and make her an author, even though I've never read a book in my life. However, little did I know that by doing this I've managed to put closure on my childhood abuse and also control my depression through writing, to not only be able to lead a normal life, but to do it with a genuine smile on my face because I'm in control of my mental health. But I've never been able to put closure on the guilt which I still live with to this day, that other people suffered because I never spoke out earlier. I've now wrote four books under completely different mentally challenging times and have developed different strategies for using writing to help me through mentally, which I'm going to share with you. Closure, distraction, both simultaneously for when the pain is really bad, and finally for when I'm perfectly fine up top but my work mates are suffering.

Now what's that saying, "Everyone's got a book inside them." Here's mine!

Chapter 1

I promise to tell the truth, the whole truth, and nothing but the truth.

One thing which I've recently learnt the hard way is not to bottle things up inside you, and to get it out sooner rather than later, before it comes back to bite you on the backside. So I'm now going to confess, and ask for forgiveness from Richard and Judy, and all of the production team from This Morning. For any pain and suffering which my actions may have caused them back in the late eighties or early nineties. When one morning they arrived at work only to find that their weather map was missing some of its famous landmarks.

Here's the true story of how they disappeared, and I know it's true, because I was the instigator.

A group of us had decided to go to Hartley's Wine Bar in the Albert Dock for a good old-fashioned lad's night out. It was a posh place and there was about eight of us, all smartly dressed and eager to impress the posh Hartley's totty as we used to call it. I can't remember exactly who ventured into town with me that night, I know Harry was there though. He was god's gift to women and would use his boy band looks along with his gleaming smile to swoop on his target, then he'd use his silver tongue to charm them, before they swiftly departed into the night. I can remember Big Bob, Tiny, and myself, wobbling at the bar, commenting on how Harry must be losing his charm as he'd been talking to the same lady all night. Then within what seemed like seconds, but we were steaming so it was probably quite a bit longer. Harry was nowhere to be seen and the bouncers had started to ask everyone to leave. Whilst outside we tried in vain to find the rest of our party, sadly to no avail, and after failing to secure a lady friend for the night, I was in the mood for mischief.

That's when I asked my fellow future partners in crime, whether they'd like to come with me for a party on This Mornings Weather Map. They didn't need much persuading, and before long we found ourselves standing high up on the quay wall, staring down at our destination. The only problem stopping us from partying, was figuring out a way to cross the large body of water that lay between the map and us. As I led the way and climbed down the quayside steps as best I could, after consuming at least ten pints and a couple of Vodka's. My eyes lit up at the sight of a boat next to a jetty. Sadly, when I got to it, I found out it was padlocked. This didn't bother Tiny, and he made his way to the end of the jetty to figure out if he could jump the ten plus feet of water, and land safely on the map. I egged him on and told him he could do it, despite him being the shortest of us at a measly 5ft 6. However, he was the most athletically built out of us. He'd not long been out of the Army, his last tour had been of Northern Ireland, and he definitely suffered from small man's syndrome.

The jetty must have been about ten-foot-long, fifteen at the most, so Tiny made his way to the quayside wall, turned around and went for it. Big Bob and me were screaming our heads off shouting, "go on Tiny, you can do it." Then we started to wet ourselves laughing when we heard the splash as we witnessed his body rise to the surface. He was a good two foot short of making it. Next it was my turn, and I was determined to do it, confident that I would with having longer legs on my 6ft frame. I started off from the same position as Tiny and sprinted as fast as I could. Then when I got to the end of the jetty I leapt into the air as high as I could, and I can remember my legs still running in mid-air. Then as gravity started to take over, I stopped running and spread my right leg as far forward as I could, and my toes made it. Regretfully the rest of my body didn't. So, Tiny had to give me a helping hand from the drink. The two of us were like a couple of drowned rats, but we'd made it to the party. Not wanting to let Big Bob miss out on the action we assured him he could do it. Only knowing full well with his excess body tissue, along with his asthma, he didn't stand a chance. However, while me and Tiny observed from the map's edge, Big Bob took his run before he leapt into the air, and somehow, he made it. Sadly, he still got soaked as when he landed right in front of us, Tiny and me simultaneously pushed backwards on a shoulder each before we gave him a helping hand out of the drink. Sorry Big Bob.

The three of us were doing a very good job of making in rain in Cornwall, when we decided to re-enact Fred's daily jump across the Irish Sea. Luckily, we all made it. Then after a good five minutes of prancing around whilst we partied, we decided on securing a souvenir or two as a momentum of the occasion. Hence the original Stonehenge and Lowestoft Lighthouse disappeared from the map that night, and for that I'm truly sorry. After we'd prized the landmarks from their location, we managed to swim back to the jetty and keep hold of them safely, although I must say I was a bit disappointed with the quality of Stonehenge compared to the lighthouse, wire gauze and paper mashie as opposed to a quality hand-crafted wooden piece.

Luckily, we managed to hail a black cab whose driver didn't mind us soaking the back of it, whilst we enlightened him on our mischievous adventure as we paraded our trophies. Big Bob was nominated to be their custodian, but they didn't stay in his possession for very long. The following morning I got a knock on the door from the plod, it was on an unrelated matter, but Big Bob got wind that I'd been lifted and was going to throw the evidence in the bin. When Tiny heard of this he flipped, he'd already got it in his head that Lowestoft Lighthouse would make a brilliant ornament in his snake tank, which would double up as a climbing frame for its inhabitants. That's where it stayed until Tiny moved away, but before he did, he sold his snakes, complete with their tank and it still contained Lowestoft Lighthouse. When he told the new owner the story of where it had come from, he burst into fits of laughter and was convinced that it was a wind-up. I often wonder where it is now. Sadly though, due to the poor quality of Stonehenge, nobody wanted it, and it did end up in the bin.

However, Richard and Judy, despite having just confessed to a crime which has left the viewers of This Morning, and yourselves baffled for decades. I hereby plead Not Guilty on the grounds of diminished responsibility, and after you've examined my evidence, I'm sure you'll agree.

Chapter 2

A little bit about me

I'm now a divorced 49-year-old man who lives alone and only has one true friend who sadly lives 400 miles away, and it just happens to be Tiny. He's the only other person from the working hard and playing even harder period in my life who I keep in contact with. The rest of our motley crew are now just distant memories, some good, some bad, but recollections which I'll always have. However, for years I'd buried the memories of my childhood abuse very deep in the back of my brain, by smoking cannabis since I was eighteen years of age. But had never been able to put closure on it. This was something which came back to bite me on the bum in the early summer of 2011, whilst the happy celebrations of everyone taking their turn wearing my 'Bubbles' from little Britain outfit at my recent fortieth party, were still fresh in my mind. Then one night after a hard day's work at my Van Sales Business, when I got home to my family, Jane my wife, was in the bath, my daughter Hope was in bed and my stepson Tony on his X-box. So, I decided to have a little bit of quiet time in the living room and I did something that I very rarely did. Read the local rag.

The pages were full of adverts displayed next to a small story. Then about six pages in, I read something that started my successful life on a downward spiral in which I lost everything, marriage, family, home, business, and friends.

Which culminated at the end of July 2019, when less than two months after I'd been within seconds of ending my own life, I came within one hour away from being homeless. With the only option to move back into my childhood home, where my mother had also recently passed away.

In the paper I read a story about the man from my childhood being sent to prison for possessing child pornography. Immediately guilt ran through my body as my brain thought that if only, I'd have spoken up all of those years ago, then others wouldn't have gone through the same pain and suffering in their life as I have, especially when you're trying your best to deal with it and child abuse is constantly mentioned in the news. My successful life was rocked and over the next few days, I finally came up with the courage to report him to the police. I'll be honest my nerves were shattered with all the guilt which I was feeling, and I was extremely apprehensive when I called. I found myself questioning whether they'd believe me or not, thus causing me more anxiety and stress.

Initially my call was handled by a man in the control centre who took down all my details, and he informed me that he'd pass my complaint over to the historic child abuse team who would call me back. They did the following day. It was a lady, Sarah. She was lovely, very sympathetic and understanding towards my complaints and she made arrangements for me to meet her a few days later at a local police station to be interviewed in the special room for victims like me. These were long agonising days as I relived what I'd gone through in order to give the police as much information as possible, so they'd take me seriously and prosecute him.

As I pulled up outside the interview room, which was located in an old, converted police house, I was determined to tell them everything in order to get him convicted and hopefully help me put closure on this horrible chapter in my life. As I walked through the door it looked just like the ones which I'd seen on the telly. Homely looking with plain carpets, curtains, wallpaper, and pictures on the wall. It was well lit by the sunlight beaming through the large window shining down on the fake flowers, brightening up the wooden coffee table. A light brown couch was positioned at an angle to the right of the window, with another one to the left. These took up most of the floorspace. Each wall had a CCTV camera situated upon it, and the wall adjacent to the door housed a mirrored window concealing more camera's, recording equipment, and of course detectives. I was greeted by a ginger haired lady who introduced herself as Lisa before she beckoned me to take a seat on the couch to the right. I was confused as I was expecting to be interviewed by Sarah. Lisa explained that the case had now been passed to her, then she asked me a few mandatory questions before inviting me to tell all. I did, I couldn't get it out fast enough. I'm not going to tell you the graphic details, just the background of my abuse.

It started in 1982, I was eleven and had just began senior school, easily led, quite often bullied, and called a tramp. I was the youngest of four, the only boy but my mum's favourite, and for that reason my sisters christened me with the nickname 'Golden Balls'. Outside of school I'd become quite bored since my best friend Frank had moved away the previous year. Luckily, two of my sisters had joined the local Sea Cadet unit some time ago and were having fun, so I asked my Mum if I could join too. However, you had to be 12, but my Mum helped in the canteen so she had a word with the Commanding Officer, who agreed that I could, but I wouldn't be insured to shoot a gun until I was 12. I was made up. At last I'd have something to do, and for the first six months I put my heart and soul into it, thoroughly enjoying myself, despite acquiring the nickname 'Fishy'. Due to quite often coming to parade straight from my part time job, peeling spuds after school in the same fish and chip shop where my Mum worked.

Then just before Christmas, a new officer appeared who was home for three months on shore leave from his job in the merchant navy. David Frances Taylor. A smartly dressed man with a moustache, about 5ft 8 in height and stocky. Over the final few parades before the Christmas break, David had been instructing a lot of the classes which I'd been attending, and he spent a lot of time helping me advance my seamanship skills. In order for me to take the career path which I'd chosen, to join the Royal Navy. Then on the final parade he asked me whether I'd like to go on a hike with him during the break, so he could teach me some map reading skills. I agreed, and over the next two weeks I went on four different walks in the countryside with what seemed a very genuine, kind, and caring person, I learnt lots of new skills along the way and received lots of free hiking equipment from him. He never touched me once, but he did take an awful lot of photographs.

Then come January, after he'd gained my family's trust following his regular visits to our house, partying over the Christmas period. On the next walk, he offered me money for nudes. Regretfully, I agreed and over the course of the rest of his shore leave, we'd spend every weekend either in my bedroom, or hiking in the woods. Him taking photographs of me at every available opportunity, whilst I thought of the nice things which I could buy with the £20. Then it all stopped when he went back to sea, and I found myself lonely and isolated again, as a lot of the other Sea Cadets had started to keep a distance from me since I'd formed such a close bond with an officer, and I was still getting bullied at school. Sadly, the only thing which I had to look forward to was David returning from sea.

When he did some months later at a Friday night parade, he made a beeline straight for me and wasted no time whatsoever in inviting me for a walk the following day.

Needless to say, I agreed and on it the £20 for photographs advanced to £40 for contact. The rate which it remained at for the next five years as he got his grubby little hands on me at every available opportunity. He didn't care whether it was in the safety of my bedroom, or the risky situation of the bushes whilst other people were walking nearby in the countryside. He just wanted to get his little kick. It only stopped when I ran away to my dream job in the Royal Navy. However, it turned out to be a nightmare. I didn't even last three months, as being in such close proximity to so many men made me feel uncomfortable and question my sexuality. Sadly, I then found myself jobless back in civvy street, finding the only way that I could convince myself that I wasn't gay, was to have sex with as many women as possible. Luckily, I got a job as a night porter in a posh hotel, and I was that lonely, I'd talk to anyone.

Once I'd finished going into great detail in the interview, I felt relieved that finally, I'd told someone the whole story. You see, I'd told very few people over the years. None of my family knew, only my wife, and strange as it may seem, a few strangers who I'd encountered over the years who'd also suffered similar to me, and it just came out in conversation. It's like we could both sense what each other had been through. Believe you me, It's a freaky feeling. Lisa then wrapped up the interview by telling me how brave I'd been and that she'd start to make some enquiries and keep me informed as to her progress. Then on my way home I thought things would finally start to get better. How wrong I was.

Chapter 3

The road to court

Now I'd finally spoken up and it was out, I took a couple of days to ponder the best way to tell my relatives. I knew my Mum would take it really badly for failing to protect her 'Golden Balls', and that my Dad probably wouldn't believe me as he used to have a pint with him, and I was a troublesome teen. That troublesome, I spent my eighteenth birthday behind bars. So I decided it was best to just come straight out with it, but to do it when they were both together, Which I did, and it broke my Mum's heart as she sobbed away, which in turn filled my body with more guilt for upsetting her with my news. She had to have extensive counselling after I told her and ever since the day I did, my Mum didn't seem the same. My Dad took it better, and said something like, "I'm ever so sorry," and knowing him he probably invited me for a pint. My sisters were very understanding and supportive when they found out.

Over the course of the next few months the guilt which I'd been feeling inside intensified and I was struggling to cope mentally, my life was starting to crumble away. I'd lost interest in my business; my marriage was starting to crack, and I was generally in a bad way. But I wouldn't seek help. Instead I chose to do it my way. Keep myself busy whilst I bury my head in the sand and carry on as my normal laughing and joking self, until eventually it went away. It doesn't, and take it from me, the longer you leave it until you put closure on something, the harder it hits you when it comes back to bite you on the bum until you do. Luckily, I've learnt how I can do this easily through writing and I'll share my methods later in case you want to have a go yourself.

During this time contact from the police had been little and infrequent to say the least. Firstly about a month after my interview I was informed by Lisa that she'd found him in prison, and conducted an interview were his only comment was indeed 'No Comment'. So she'd be continuing with her enquiries. This rocked me further, secretly I'd been hoping that he'd do the right thing and plead guilty to save me the horrendous ordeal of having to go to court to testify. Nevertheless, even though I could feel myself spiralling downwards, no matter what, I was determined to have my day in court and watch him walk down the steps to prison. Even though frequently reliving the trauma which I'd suffered on a daily basis was causing my mental state to decline further, thus causing my business and marriage to fall apart.

The next few months I became even worse, and I'd totally taken my eye off the ball. I was walking around in a world of my own, consumed with guilt from within. Desperate to find a way to make it go away, too proud to ask anyone for help, and the only thing which I found did, was by helping people in any way I could. Once the guilt had set in over taking money instead of speaking out, money was irrelevant to me. Sadly, I got my fingers burnt several times and lost thousands, as customers would come in and give me a sob story about how they needed a van for work, so they could go out and earn a wage to provide for their family, but they didn't have enough money. So I'd feel sorry for them and agree for them to pay what they had up front, and the balance directly into my bank on a monthly payment plan. Interest free. Most of them made the first payment then defaulted, and I couldn't be bothered going knocking on their doors chasing the rest. I'd quite happily take the loss rather than create any more stress in my life. Soon after this I realised that my cash reserves were quickly disappearing, and for the first time I seriously considered downsizing my business and going back to my friends farm where I started back in 2008, but in order for me to do this, I'd have to make my four loyal employees who had become friends, redundant. This was something that I didn't want to do.

Then in September things at home hit rock bottom, and neither of us could take the strain anymore, so Jane instructed me to leave. I was devastated, we'd been together for fourteen years. It started off as a one-night stand, she was a young single mum who'd just left her husband, to me a 'damsel in distress', who just happened to be a good friend of mine's sister. You see I'm a true Pisces, a hopeless romantic who sees the good in everyone and the world through rose tinted glasses, and here was my chance to be a 'Knight in shining armour' and rescue my 'Damsel in distress' before we fell madly in love with each other.

15

We did. However, now we'd fallen out of love, so I understood her reasons for kicking me out and left without a fight. Hopeful that it was only a blip. I decided not to rent anywhere straight away, and I certainly didn't want to put any more stress or strain on my family by asking to stay at theirs. So I grabbed the folding metal camp bed along with my sleeping bag, some pillows, a rucksack full of clothes, and moved into the messy portacabin office at my premises. What a scary experience that was, the room was illuminated by the streetlights shining through the wafer thin blinds, while the noise from the rowdy drunks and the main road traffic kept me awake, and then when it did go quiet, all I could hear was the sound of rustling in the bushes behind.

On two separate nights somebody attempted to break in, and I had all of the keys to the vans with me, as well as the ones for the locked gates to get them out of. I was determined that I wasn't going down without a fight and grabbed a big screwdriver from on top of the filing cabinet and started screaming that the police were on their way. Luckily, my shouting stopped them in their tracks, and they scarpered. Then within four days Jane had calmed down so I was reunited with my family. Things still weren't right at home, I was miserable, as was my wife, and the kids very rarely ventured out of their bedrooms, fearful whether they'd walk into one of our frequent heated arguments or get the frosty atmosphere instead.

The burglars did get in the following week, but they didn't take anything, they only left a bloody big mess. Oddly though, about a week later we got a visit from a well-built male who was representing a local security firm, asking whether we'd like to pay to have the premises protected after our break in. I found this very strange as it wasn't common knowledge. But luckily for me, my mate Big Bill, who worked for me as and when required, just happened to walk onto the pitch at the same time. Luckily, he recognised the man, so he took control of the situation by shaking him by the hand before they had a brief chat, prior to him departing. We never had any more trouble after that, and I never worried about any more break ins. Big Bill had only come to ask if he could live in his horsebox at the back of my pitch, as he'd been booted out by his girlfriend. How's that for timing.

For the rest of the year things went steadily downhill, my mind was firmly fixated with the police investigation, and what I found very stressful was the 'all or nothing' approach from them. I'd get two or three phone calls within a couple of days, and then nothing for months. So I fought on as best I could until January 2012, when I received a call from Lisa, telling me that she had to see me urgently. I was at auction when I took the call and I told her that I wouldn't be back till 9 PM so it would have to wait until the following day. Lisa stated that it couldn't wait until then and it had to be today, therefore a 9 PM meeting at my house was arranged. That call totally wrecked by brain, and with hindsight I should have gone home straight away. But

I didn't, and I made six very bad purchases that day, putting even more strain and pressure not only on my finances, but also my mental state. Regrettably, I'd already spent all of my dwindling stock money, and I was taking a gamble as I was determined to turn things around, so I put the full £40000 on my personal credit cards.

I arrived home about 8.30 PM, then whilst sitting in the living room Jane and I hardly said a word to each other, she had a glass of wine in her hand, I had a bottle of beer in mine, and we just sat staring out of the window, watching for the police to arrive. They were late and didn't turn up until 9.15. It had been a long agonising forty-five minutes sat in virtual silence, whilst the atmosphere thickened. As soon as I spotted Lisa getting out I immediately made for the front door and showed her the way to the living room before I offered her a drink. She declined and got straight down to the point. "He's been released from prison after completing his sentence and is living in a halfway house. However, he's prepared to plead guilty to sample charges relating to when you were over the age of thirteen, if we drop the charges for when you were younger."

This brought relief in one way, but pain in another. Relief that finally people would believe me and that I wouldn't have to go through the ordeal of a trial. But I was saddened as I knew these charges were a lot more serious than the ones which he'd admit to, as such, they also carried a much bigger custodial sentience. I thought the reprieve of not having to attend a trial would be the end of my suffering and I'd finally be able to get my closure. Sadly, those six bad purchases came back to bite me on the backside, and I lost thousands on them. The bank balance wasn't healthy, my stock had dwindled from carrying forty vans, to twenty, with less than ten in a saleable condition. Then in April I realised that I had to get my head out of the sand and come up with a plan to turn things around. Regrettably, it involved making my friends and employees redundant by slashing my £12000 a month overheads, whilst I went back to Stuart's farm.

Chapter 4

One step forward, two steps back

Things started to get better for me now I'd slashed my overheads to £3000 a month, but in doing so, it meant I had to do a lot more of the preparation work myself. On the muddy soil patch which I rented on Stuart's farm. This along with all of the time spent at auction buying stock, meant I was rarely at home, and even when I was, my time was taken up with paperwork, advertising, VAT returns and all of the other activities associated with being a one-man operation. I wasn't going forward financially very much and was surviving by paying the minimum amount to my creditors each month. But I'd taken a lot of the pressure from my shoulders and I was still providing for my family. However no one knew how ripped apart I felt inside. Or the horrible memories my mind was reliving whenever I had any spare thinking time. Then not long after I'd moved back to the farm Lisa called to say he'd pleaded guilty in magistrates court, but they'd referred it to crown court as the maximum sentence they could give was six months. So she'd keep me informed. Finally some good news and my mental state improved, knowing justice was soon to be served, and I could finally gain closure by watching in court as his sentence is handed out, before he walks from the dock to a prison cell.

Then by September, when his day in court finally arrived, things had vastly improved both at work and at home. Life was much better in general, apart from the morning of his court case that was, when I woke up extremely nervous and anxious before I had a major wobble and couldn't face seeing him again. Luckily, I decided to head to court anyway after reassuring myself I could back out at any time if these thoughts continued. I met Lisa outside the courtroom at 10.30 as agreed, and she asked whether I still wanted to go in for the sentencing before reassuring me that it was alright if I wasn't up to it. As I'd been brave enough already to speak out after all of these years. That must have hit a note with me because all of the anxiety disappeared from inside, and now I didn't just want to witness his freedom taken away, I wanted to look him in the eyes before it was. Then just before 11 AM I got my chance when a lady in a suit, who was carrying a lot of paperwork in a folder, approached Lisa, and told her "we're on," before swiftly departing. I led the way and opened the courtroom door for Lisa, who in turn led me to our seats behind the dock, to its right.

He was sat in it, next to a prison guard. But where we'd sat wasn't close enough for me, I'd come this far and I didn't want to stare into his eyes from a distance, I wanted it to be really close so that he'd remember it for the rest of his life. Therefore, I stood up and told Lisa I was sitting right behind the dock before repositioning myself. Lisa followed and I can't describe how I felt finding myself sat less than two foot away from him. I didn't feel angry though, I think I was just taken aback by the whole thing. Listening to the legal teams speaking to the court, before witnessing the judge sat in his wig and gown, high on his bench above the court, with the crown towering over him. As he told the court about the trauma and pain his actions had caused to a young boy who'd kept it bottled up for years, until he'd been brave enough to come forward after reading a story in a newspaper. The judge then sentenced him to thirty months in prison, and when he did, I got my golden opportunity as he turned around and looked right at me. So I gave him a stare he'll never forget before he was led away.

Still taken aback with what I'd just done, outside the courtroom Lisa and myself said our goodbyes by giving each other a big hug. Then she asked how I was feeling, so I told her about how the 'all or nothing' contact from the police had caused lots of strain on my mental health during the process. From her reply I subsequently learnt that these were standard practices, designed to weed out the liars. Both satisfied with the result, we went our separate ways and for the next few days we were both featured in the news. She was the detective who'd put him behind bars, and me, the unknown brave little boy who was now a man, appealing for any victims of historic abuse to speak out now, rather than to go through the pain of suffering in silence. It was a happy ending for all, Lisa got her conviction, and I could finally get my closure. Only little did I know it'd be a long roller coaster of a ride until I did.

My first step to closure came with a visit to my house by a lady representing a local rape and victim support scheme. She was lovely and made me feel quite at ease, the conversation flowed, and it was agreed that I would try a course of counselling, commencing the following week. After her visit my mood improved and I was looking forward to the challenges of life again. My wife and I were getting on, business was ticking along, and I was finally going to get rid of the guilt from within, which was making me feel sad inside. Then my first counselling session came along, it was with a different lady, and we tried to speak openly about my life, but for the first time, someone who has the mentality, 'I'll talk to anyone because I don't know the last time someone spoke to them, and you never know where it might lead', didn't want to talk. My mood dipped after my first session, but I was determined to give it another go, and in our next meeting I started to open up, and we went back to why I ran away to the Royal Navy.

I was sixteen when my abuse ended, and I hadn't tried my best in school as I'd already got a lifelong career lined up. So off I toddled into the big wide world to hopefully put an end to a horrible chapter in my life. I was full of beans and determined to make the best of it. Which I did. During my basic training at HMS Raleigh, and due to the seamanship skills which I'd learnt over my years in the Sea Cadets, I was given the responsibility of becoming 'Class Leader' and being in charge of my class of thirty. I was also the youngest. I thoroughly enjoyed my basic training and for the first time in my life, I felt like I fitted in. I put so much effort into my Naval career, I was awarded the Raleigh Medal for the highest individual marks in training. Sadly, when I moved to HMS Sultan for my next stage of training, I felt uncomfortable sharing a dorm in close proximity with three other men, and I just wanted out. So I did what I always do. I ran from my problem instead of dealing with it, and that's why I ended up becoming a night porter. Then whilst working there one night, I got talking to a well-dressed man who was sat alone at the bar, and I noticed his car keys positioned on it, his keys were dwarfed by a big Mercedes keyring. We got talking and I asked him what he did for a living, he said he was a car salesman, so I asked him what it was like. "Long hours, but if you're good at it you can make a decent living." Two days later I was selling cars, and it turned out that I was good at it, everyone used to say I could sell sand to the Arab's. Then I became sad within after reliving my short Naval career, and started to wonder what my life would be like now if I had stayed in. I'd be coming up for retirement soon, on a full pension. I'd have travelled the world and would have almost certainly advanced in the ranks.

Then about half an hour after my session had ended, I received a call from a probation service lady, wanting to arrange to meet with me, and discuss keeping me informed of his whereabouts on a regular basis. We agreed a suitable time, and I specifically made sure I had no work commitments that day. Then about thirty minutes before she was due, she called and said she was running late and asked if she could come a bit later. When I told her it didn't matter as I'd taken the day off work, so she could come anytime. She apologised to me and said that due to cutbacks she really didn't have enough time to come and see me at all. But assured me that I would be kept well informed of his whereabouts, to prevent me accidentally bumping into him. Sadly, I never heard from them again, and I did bump into him. He was carrying a camera around children. You'll find out my reactions later in my story.

Then the third session didn't go very well, and I was getting angry with the counsellors questioning. I don't know what had come over me, I'm normally always calm and relaxed with the attitude, 'it'll all sort itself out in the wash, so what's the point in worrying.' But here I found myself getting very angry, and I told the lady that I didn't need any more counselling, because it was making me feel worse. So I was going to do it my way. Sadly, my way wasn't working and before long my mental state had deteriorated further, my marriage had started to crack again, my business was suffering heavily, and I couldn't take it anymore. So I went to the doctor's for help. Where I found myself diagnosed with depression and advised that I needed to go on some tablets. I'll be honest with you, even though I felt ashamed of admitting that I had mental health problems and had heard so many horror stories about being on anti's for life, I was relieved once I had and willing to try anything which would help make me better. However, after taking them for a few days, I started to get suicidal thoughts constantly in my head. So I stopped taking them and knew that if I was going to beat my depression, then

I'd have to find another way of doing it. I did find a way, but it took me another seven agonising years in which I lost everything, and it was only after instead of taking my own life, I decided to write in my late mother's name as tribute, so her name would live on forever. That I've found out my true self. What a Roller coaster my life has been on since I made that choice, only this time a positive one for a change. But before I tell you the story of how I stumbled across using writing to control my mental health and lead a perfectly normal life. I'll continue to tell you my story of the journey to the bottom.

Chapter 5

It's a long way down

Now what I haven't told you so far, is that not long after I'd stared that man in the eyes, it wasn't only my story which was featured in the news. Jimmy Saville was. Heavily, and every time I heard a news report on the TV or radio, or looked at the front page of a paper, it brought everything back and made me feel worse. It had that much media coverage there was no getting away from it. So, a few months after I'd come off the medication and quit the counselling, I was lost. My finances had dwindled to a £30000 overdraught, business was slack, and I was in real danger of going bankrupt. Luckily, my Mum and Dad very kindly offered to let me have my inheritance early, by taking out a lifetime mortgage on their house. It wasn't a large sum, £20000 but it was enough for me to buy half-a-dozen vans, and I was up and running again. Over the course of the next six months I was flying, things were good at home, business was booming so I took on another pitch. Only this one had somewhere to paint my own vans.

That was how I made my money. By going to the auctions and buying mechanically sound but rough on the bodywork ex Royal Mail vans. They were cheap, and nobody else wanted them. The auctions loved me for buying them. I was even on the free breakfast list. So I'd buy as many as I could, then repair the bodywork and paint them before I sold them cheap. But I'd also advertise that I'd paint them any colour included in the price. People came from all over the country to buy them, and always left satisfied with the job.

This good spell lasted for about 18 months, and it was a happy time, the business was going forward. I had two employees, and I'd started to offer finance. At home we'd even been on a family holiday to Majorca, and we had a thoroughly good time. Sadly, not long after we got back, we had to get Ollie, our chocolate Labrador put down to end his suffering. He was a brave dog, and only ended up with us by mistake as we'd gone to a breeder in Wales to get a Chocolate bitch to mate with Colin and Jasper, our black and golden boys. When we got there Ollie was the liveliest of the bunch and wouldn't stop pulling on my pants. The breeder checked it's bit's and confirmed it was a female before he took our money and we departed. Then on the way home whilst Jane was holding the, as yet unnamed puppy on her lap, she discovered it had a button mushroom. Good job really, because I only found out at a later date that you can only breed a chocolate lab with the same colour.

But we always think that Ollie was destined to be ours, as after only a few months, he was diagnosed with severe hip dysplasia that would cost thousands in surgery, and we didn't have it, nor insurance. Luckily for us, the vet who we used had just successfully treated a small dog with the same condition, by simply cutting of the ball at the end of his leg socket and let the scar tissue grow to hold it all together. The vets told us that they didn't know if it would work on a big dog like Ollie, but we gambled and gave it a go. I'm so glad we did as Ollie, with his wobbly backside, soon became everybody's favourite. Getting him put to sleep was the end of an era for us, he was the last of our full set of Lab's. Jasper our Golden one developed cancer and had to get put down. Sadly, this was only seven months after we'd lost Colin, his sibling, who'd eaten some food baited with poison whilst out on our nightly walk and was dead within 24 hours. I've got so many happy memories made with those dogs, and no matter whatever the weather, or time, they always got their nightly walk.

Things started to go downhill at home from then on, and in the summer of 2014 my Dad had a heart attack and stroke, and as a result, he developed vascular dementia. You could see the change in him straight away, confused, and forgetful whilst struggling to hold a sensible conversation. Me and my Dad never spent a lot of time together during my childhood, he was always working, or in the pub, and I was busy with Sea Cadets or David. One good thing which did come out of his conviction, was that for the first time in years, my father and I developed a really good bond. He loved spending all of his free time at my pitch, as he said it gave him something to do, rather than sit at home being bored. All of the staff loved having him around, because his mannerisms made him a very funny man. We used to go to the auction in Leeds every Monday, and whilst sat next to each other, we chatted none-stop all of the way, making up for lost time. Then when we arrived he'd head straight for the canteen to get his greasy fry-up before he'd have a walk around the vans whilst inspecting them for any damage which I might have missed. Once I'd finished buying for the day, he got to drive home in the luxuries of the Range Rover, whilst I brought home a bright red Royal Mail van.

Then in August, and still rocked by my dad's ill health, I got a phone call from HM Revenue and Customs, wanting to make an appointment to inspect my books for the past 7 years. My world had just fallen apart, and I was scared. These people had the power to effectively end your life if they exercised their right to seize your assets, and my paperwork system consisted of putting all of my receipts and invoices into the relevant bin bags, and when it was time to complete the quarterly VAT return, they would be entered in sage in the order that they came out of the bin bag in, prior to filling. I panicked, I'd had a vat inspection back in 2006 after I'd only been self-employed for a year, and they hit me with a £300 bill for an invoice which I'd missed. So now I had to focus all of my attention firmly on making sure my books were in order, and for the next 14 days I spent every hour of the day sifting through seven years' worth of paperwork, before checking it had been entered into sage, and guess what. I found stuff that hadn't.

On the morning of the lady's visit I was absolutely crapping myself. In my weak mental state, I'd convinced myself that my world was ending today, when my assets

were froze and I was charged with defrauding the Queen.
Ever since I'd found the missing invoices, which
incidentally were both for stuff I could claim back, as well
as stuff that I owed. I'd been unsure what to do, whether to
just declare them from the start, or wait for her to find
them. I chose the latter, and after only inspecting my books
for less than ten minutes, she cautioned me, and in a stern
voice said, that because my paperwork records where not in
date order, I was now under a formal investigation as she
suspected that I was deliberately trying to defraud the
Crown, and I had 14 days to put all of my paperwork into
date order, then she'd be back. I panicked, what with all of
the worry of my Dad, and now this on top of everything
else, I could feel my mental state slipping away, while the
cracks in my marriage developed into unrepairable holes.

During the next 14 days my Dad's health deteriorated and
he'd been admitted to hospital. With all of the worry this
was causing, along with the thought of me not being able to
support my family through it, after the HMRC woman has
locked me up and thrown away the keys. I really was in a
bad place on the morning of the ladies second visit. The
doorbell rang just after ten, and I don't know how I kept it
together as I answered. I was convinced that when she
walked back out of the door, my life would be over. How
wrong I was. This stern Lady who I'd met a few weeks
earlier transformed into an angel after I'd explained the full
story behind the £20000 cash injection from my parents.
Not long after I had we went out to the gazebo for a smoke,
and when I spoke to that lady without her revenue hat on,

what a lovely down to earth woman she was; worked for the treasury for years, and had become that disillusioned in her job with all of the changes, she was just counting down the years to retirement.

She didn't stay very long when we got back in the house, probably about half an hour, until I received a phone call from my Mum, saying that my Dad was being released from hospital, and asking if I'd go and pick him up. I explained this to the revenue lady, who said it was fine as she'd seen enough, but had found some minor discrepancies. However, she reassured me that it was nothing to worry about and if I couldn't afford it, she'd put a payment plan in place. Luckily, it wasn't that much so I paid it in one. Sadly though, with all of the high's and lows of the roller coaster so far, things had become really bad at home, and within a week of getting the revenue off my back, my marriage shattered into tiny pieces when it was decided by Jane, that I was moving out forever.

Chapter 6

Look into my eyes

It was a Saturday night in early October when it ended. We both couldn't take it anymore. The arguing, glaring, staring and the horrendous atmosphere which our house contained had simply defeated us. I can remember crying my eyes out as I crammed whatever I could into our large family sized suitcase, then once I'd finished I approached Jane one last time, making sure it was what she wanted. Sadly, it was, so I put my bravest face on as I went into Tony's room, and as I shook his hand I told him I was leaving and asked him to look after his Mum and Hope for me, as he was now the man of the house. Then it was Hope's turn, as I opened her bedroom door she asked what was up. The tears were pouring down my cheeks as I hugged her tightly in my arms and told her that her Dad was moving out. She burst into tears and begged for me to stay. I told her that it was for the best as me and Mum just weren't getting on, and by me not living there didn't mean I'll love her any less, and that she'll still see me. I then went back to our bedroom to ask Jane just to say so and I wouldn't go. All I got was silence, so it was a tearful journey all of the way to my new life on my Mum's two-seater couch.

Here I stayed for a couple of weeks just to make sure Jane did want it over, before I swopped my 250-motocross bike for my mate Stan's campervan, and I moved into it on my pitch. At this point I didn't know how I was managing to keep it all together up top, and remain so happy and cheerful on the outside, whilst my insides had just been ripped apart. However, the one thing that I was missing the most, was to be able to check that Hope and Tony were safely tucked up in bed before I went to mine every night.

I was devastated that my marriage was over. I'd miss them dearly, and I didn't want my kids to come from a one parent family. When I got married I took my vows very seriously, and never wanted to get divorced. I was a firm believer that no matter what, together you'd find a way through. Sadly though, we hadn't, and I now found myself treading water in life, without any direction in it. Living in a 1980's campervan on an industrial estate on the outskirts of a very posh village, as the cold winters nights were drawing in. I only lasted about a month, the weather got to me, and it wasn't suitable for having Hope to stay over every alternate weekend, as had now been arranged. So I took the plunge and rented a small two bedroom downstairs flat. The only problem was it was thirty minutes' drive away from home, and it was tiny compared to our three-bedroom semi which had a garage and large gardens, not to mention the length of the four-car driveway. But it meant Hope could come over to stay, which she did, and on the Sunday of the first weekend that I had her, we decided to take a trip on the Mersey ferry. Starting at Seacombe, then calling at Woodside, before arriving at the Pier Head in Liverpool, where we'd planned to get off the ferry and conduct a tour of the museum, prior to returning on the boat to Seacombe later in the day.

We were having fun, and it was a sunny day, so we did a tour of spaceport first, before getting on the ferry and doing what Hope always does best. Extract money out of me for the shop. Once she'd filled her pockets with merchandise we set off for the upper deck to listen to the guided tour, as we viewed the beautiful sight of the Liverpool waterfront. Then as we were approaching Liverpool Hope wanted to be the first off the boat, so we raced to the gangway and observed as the ferry came ever closer to the Pier Head. The crewman hoist the lines overboard to his colleague standing ashore who was waiting to catch it, and before I knew it, the gangway was lowered. Then my body froze with fear when I witnessed who was standing in the front of the que, waiting to board, and he was stood amongst children while carrying a camera.

My fear turned to anger, and I just wanted to rip his head off. Luckily for me, I had hold of Hope's hand, and I squoze it tightly before I pulled her towards me as we exited the vessel. As we walked past him I looked in his direction, hopeful I would catch his eye so I could give him the same stare as I had in court. Sadly, I didn't, and words can't describe how I was feeling as we made our way to the museum, or as we were walking around it. Knowing he was on the ferry acting like an innocent tourist, only really he'd be taking pictures of children who were out enjoying the sunshine with their loved ones.

Then whilst walking around the museum, my mind had become firmly fixated on how I was going to react if we saw him on our way back. Suddenly, my thoughts switched to. 'I don't just want to see him; I want to whisper in his ear before I look him in the eye to show him that I'm not scared of him anymore. Then hopefully he'll be frightened and run off home so no more pictures would be taken by him that day'. I made sure we got back to the ferry with sufficient time to ensure we were at the front of the que when the ferry docked, and luckily for me, he was the first one off.

I was holding Hope tightly in my hand while he had a big grin on his face, as he walked towards me with his camera hanging around his neck. Then when I was stood right next to the barrier he got within inches of me, so I leant towards him and whispered in his ear. "Do you still like playing with little boys because guess what! Little boys grow up." He turned his head to look me in the eyes before I witnessed the look of fear in his, and after I gave him the same stare as I had in court, he scarpered as fast as he could. Then for the first time, I wasn't afraid of him anymore. I was shocked and felt let down by the system. However, I was still reliving the trauma his actions caused on a daily basis, thus causing my depression to deepen.

My marriage break up along with all of the other things which had happened recently, rocked my confidence and my business was really starting to suffer. What hadn't helped was that earlier in the year I'd expanded and rented bigger premises specifically for a paint shop. I'd also invested in a booth. Things were great at first and it looked like it was a good decision, until Pete the Painter started to have problems at home, and he became unreliable. So I now found myself with the added financial pressure and no one to paint my vans. I was sinking. Fast. But then by Christmas things started to pick up at home, and on Christmas day I was reunited with my family after Jane and I decided to give it another go. It was lovely to come home to my family again, and to be able to check on Hope and Tony before I went to bed. However, it did leave an empty flat.

Then just after Christmas one of Tony's relations was made homeless, and he needed somewhere to live. His name was Charlie, a computer programmer, and I saw my opportunity to settle a score with a company that had grown into a member of the FTSE club. For legal reasons I'm not going to mention the said company, as they've got a lot more money than me. So I feel that I must make it clear that I'm not making any accusations with what I'm about to share with you, as far as I'm concerned everything's purely coincidental, and the rest is just my thoughts. Apart from the meetings which actually did take place.

Back in 2005 when I was buying a lot of cars from the public for the garage who I was working for, I spotted a gap in the market for a website, whereby a member of the public who was selling their car could input it's details, to receive the contact details of multiple trade buyers who were willing to make them an offer. I didn't charge them a fee for selling, nor buying. I was to make my money by charging the dealers a monthly subscription for their listing.

Now before and during the time my idea was in development, I just happened to be selling cars to a very large car supermarket group, and I'd struck up a friendly rapport with a man called Ted. Once I'd told him my idea he'd quite often ask how my new venture was coming along, then take a keen interest in my reply, and all the while I was telling him what a massive market the cash for cars one was. Knowing that if I had someone with their buying power on board, it would boost my websites chances of success. In fact in October 2005 when development was complete, and I launched it, they were one of the first dealers to buy a car from it. I was buzzing, it was working, and for the first few months things were going great. That was until the very same car supermarket launched their own cash for cars website. I've since found out afterwards that within a couple of months of informing Ted about my new venture, their domain name was registered.

Chapter 7

I got them talking

Anyway it's now January 2015 and by pure chance a computer programmer needs somewhere to live, and I've got somewhere. A deal was struck whereby he could live there rent free as part of his wage, whilst he built me a website. Now, a lot of you may not know this, but a lot of the big cash for cars websites are actually owned by companies who have sister companies which are auction houses, and all they do is buy from the general public before they sell them via the said auctions to the trade and public alike. So my idea for a website took there model of inputting your vehicle's reg to get a quote, only it gave you multiple instant offers from dealers who were willing to pay you more and save on the auction fees. As I'd built in for each dealer their own cash for cars website for free. It was like a price comparison site for selling your car. It was a simple concept whereby it would take both the buyers, and sellers away from the big boys by giving every motor dealer the same concept which they had created.

It was a mammoth project, and it took up a lot of my time, but due to my history of the market, I had an investor keen to invest from an early stage, after kicking himself for not investing back in 2005. All I had to do to get my big payday was to get a fully functional working website. So as I'm sure you can appreciate, here I was with my golden opportunity to give my family a much better life, as we've all heard about these small companies who get bought out for millions by the big boys, because they see them as that much of a threat.

Now I didn't want a repeat of what happened back in 2005, but I knew that in order for me to stand a chance of succeeding, I had to come up with a way of getting the big boys who could easily pinch my idea and develop it, tied up on a confidentiality agreement. Then after a couple of months of successful development we had a working prototype. It wasn't pretty on the eye, and it was a long way from being complete, but it worked. So while the developer spent some time working on the design, I set about taking the big boys out of the way. As it happens this was quite easy to do as the only auctioneer who I trusted, had just been made redundant by one of the auctions who did have a cash for cars website, and luckily for me, he was now working for the one who didn't. It didn't take me long to convince him that this was an easy way for his auction to get a foothold in the cash for cars market, and within weeks, I found myself having a meeting with his managing director, demonstrating my idea. He wasn't impressed, he said it would take business away from his core business, and for that reason he asked me to leave. Which I did, but I did so with my confidentiality agreement tucked safely away in my briefcase.

One down two to go, so I set my sights on the company who my auction contact had recently been let go from. It didn't take much to snare them. I used the manager of the local centre to set a meeting up with one of his big bosses, so I could show them how they could take the big fish on. It worked a treat and before long I was sitting in front of a very senior boardroom member, who'd just signed my confidentiality agreement. However, he said he saw the potential in it and would get back to me. Sadly, he never did. Two down, one to go and I had no idea how I was going to get them to agree to a meet. But luckily for me, the first auction house who I approached had since decided to sell his business to the big fish and seeing as he'd signed a confidentiality agreement with me, that was them taken out of the equation.

I used to get regular phone calls from my auctioneer friend after that, and they'd always start off by him saying, "The witches of the round table have asked me to snoop on your progress, what would you like me to tell them." My answer would always be, "tell them it's coming along nicely, and we'll be launching soon." However, we weren't launching soon, and due to stock becoming harder to purchase from the auctions, I'd totally taken my eye of my key business, selling vans, and my main investor knew I was running out of money, so he was trying to get more for less. I struggled on as best I could for the rest of the year until the late summer, when my finances had diminished to such a measly state, I now found myself in the unfortunate position whereby I simply ran out of money. With the developer off the books, there was no way to finish the project, and I found myself closing the business and having to go back to driving wagons to make ends meet. This was something which I hadn't done for over twenty years.

I was lucky, I got a job only a few miles from our house pretty quickly. It was through an agency at first, until I got took on full time later in the year, working nights, on a 4 on 4 off shift pattern. But because it wasn't the best paid job in the world, I would do as much overtime as I could. I'd start at 10.30 at night, and sometimes I wouldn't finish until gone 1 PM the following day. But I'd finally plucked up the courage to tell Jane about the true extent of my financial struggle. So it was agreed that we'd sell the house and seeing as with the mortgage would be paid off once it was gone, we wouldn't have a financial association. Therefore, if we put the equity in Jane's account, then if I did end up going splat, they wouldn't be able to touch it. The house went pretty quickly, but with all of the upheaval of the move, along with our marriage simply consisting of us being ships that passed in the night, the cracks had well and truly developed. I soldiered on as best I could for the following year or so.

Then one dark November winters night in 2016, at just past midnight, I had a bizarre accident that would change my life. I went to sit on a picnic bench in the outside smoking area at work, but it was faulty; one of the supports had broken. So as a consequence when I sat on one side, my downward motion was like a see-saw effect, only with nobody siting on the other side, the bench flipped over and pinned me to the deck. I was lying there, shouting out for help. The pain from my left arm and shoulder which had taken the full force of the bench was severe. After unsuccessfully trying to wrestle the heavy bench from on top of me for about ten minutes, one of the shunter drivers noticed me and burst into laughter after he had. He found it that funny, he wouldn't help me until he took a picture.

I couldn't work after that and I had a year off on the sick before they sacked me for not being capable of doing the job which I was employed for. Even though I was only two weeks away from seeing a consultant who'd been talking about giving me a steroid injection in my shoulder, which would hopefully have me back driving again. However, if they'd have waited any longer before dismissing me, I'd have had two years' service in the bag, and with it, a lot more rights.

That was the final straw and when the insurance company sent someone out to assess me, after sitting at home rotting away for the past year, feeling useless and with no sense of purpose in life. I was diagnosed with severe depression. Luckily, the injection did work and at least I could get back to earning a living with the agency, and I was doing so as best I could in my current mental state, until early January 2018, when just shortly after Jane had lost her cousin to cancer, she told me that our marriage was over for good.

Even though I didn't want it over, I didn't hate Jane for the pain she was causing me. I mean, what sort of a husband had I been for the past year. Miserable, Moody, content with lying on the couch all of the time with no motivation at all, and ever since my accident I'd found it easier to sleep on it to. I still loved her and believed that despite everything, we could still work it out. What also hadn't helped was Jane's heavy grieving for her late cousin.

Tony moved out first in the January. He'd found himself a one bedroom flat, so it was time for him to take his next step into the big wide world. After that I tried my best to convince Jane to give it one more go, and I remained hopeful that I could right up until the day I moved them into their new house in the March. I'll always remember standing on their doorstep once everything was in, praying that this was all a bad dream, and that Jane would let me stay. That was the hardest thing I've ever done, because after a crying Hope had made me promise her that I would go back to my mums and not sleep in the car, when I walked out of the door, I knew I would be missing out on being involved in a large part of my daughter's life.

I didn't go back to my Mum's; I spent the next two nights in the rented house that we'd just vacated, as the keys weren't going back until Monday. I just wanted some time to gather my thoughts, and I found myself staring at my possessions in the corner. Thinking to myself how sad it was that after all of my efforts in life, all I've got to show for it is contained in the large family suitcase, two laptop bags, and a couple of bin bags. Not forgetting the £85000 debt which I was now in. I was also fearful of what the next chapter in my life had in store for me. Moving back into my childhood home, only this time when I did, I'd be doing so suffering from what had now well and truly turned into severe depression.

Chapter 8

It was very strange

It was only my Mum living at home now, my Dad's condition had deteriorated so much, that sadly my Mum with her chronic COPD, couldn't cope with him living at home anymore. As a result in the February of 2017, he'd been made a permanent resident of a nursing home when it was diagnosed that he didn't have medical capacity. I wasn't looking forward to moving back in, when I had a few years previously, my Dad was still at home, and seeing as they both slept in separate bedrooms, it had been the couch for me. Along with the sound of the grandfather clock ticking away all night. That house had never felt the same to me ever since I left as a teenager, I always felt uncomfortable, and sensed a strange atmosphere. I don't know why, but I did.

As soon as I let myself in my Mum gave me a great big hug, the sort that only a Mum could give, and then I couldn't get a word in edgeways, as she filled me in on the family gossip. You see, I didn't see my Mum very often, I was too busy with work, and took her for granted that she'd always be there, and she was. Right now in my hour of need, and she'd prepared a bed in my Dad's vacant bedroom. Our house was a 150-year-old three bedroom terraced, with the third bedroom being the attic. When we were growing up, my Mum and Dad had the big bedroom, a place where we would never dare to venture, uninvited.

My sister's shared the creepy attic, whereby being the only boy, I got the other bedroom all to myself. Then when my sisters moved out, I got the creepy attic, as my Mum and Dad had decided to sleep in separate bedrooms, so my Mum moved into mine. Where she's slept nightly ever since, and the attic has become the dumping ground for all of their life's clutter. I'm so glad it has because it holds horrible memories of that man too. The first night at my Mum's was strange to say the least, I cried under the quilt for most of it, trying my best to hide it from my Mum, not wanting to give her any more worry. Over the years I used to mask my sadness with a good sense of humour, and I found out that when I made people laugh and smile, it would make me do so too, and it took away the pain that I was feeling inside. Therefore, nobody knew how I was really feeling, and never suspected in any way that I had depression. Only Jane knew. I was ashamed to tell anyone else. Even my Mum.

It was hard living back in that house, and even though I never ventured into those two rooms, sometimes when you were walking up the stairs, you'd get a flashback of him walking behind you all those years ago. Ogling my backside, as wicked thoughts raced through his brain. But it was good to be spending time with Mum again, and even though I told her not to, she fussed over me. Always made me butties for work, did my washing, and I didn't have to do any housework. The only chore which I had to do, was trim her bush for her. It was that overgrown, it was getting trapped every time you closed the front door. She'd often ask me to trim her bush next time I came as I departed, knowing full well that everyone who was present would find it funny. She had a wicked sense of humour and a filthy mind, and that must be where I get mine from. I was working for an agency at the time, and staying out for days driving lorry's, long distance, and at the same time I was desperately trying to save my marriage. So sadly, I didn't get to spend as much time with her as I'd have liked. Then in the April, I was sinking fast and the time which I'd been dreading for all of the previous years had finally arrived. It was time to call the banks. Which I did, and I'm still finding them very helpful and sympathetic towards me to this day. If anybody is afraid of approaching them, don't be, they have specialist teams wanting to help.

Things were still patchy between Jane and me, but we were speaking, and I was looking after Hope at her house on the days that she was working. I was quite lucky at the time as I'd started working casually for a firm 45 minutes' drive away in Wrexham, but luckily they were screaming out for drivers, so as a result, I could pick my shifts around Jane's. It wasn't brilliant, some nights I'd start at 1 in the morning, others 4 in the afternoon, then I'd be away for three days solid. All of my hard work was getting rewarded though, I was earning good money again, and both myself and Jane wanted to see a fortune teller, so we decided on going on a family trip to Blackpool. Tony didn't want to come, so it was just Jane, Hope, and me. It was weird on the way there in the car, it just didn't feel right. I was trying my best to make them laugh, but nothing was working. Then when we got there it was straight to the arcades where we amused ourselves by spending a fortune on the slots. Then once we'd had a bite to eat and toured the attractions whilst spending a pretty packet, we headed to get our fortunes told.

The sun was shining down as the three of us strolled along the sea front, we all seemed happy. There'd been no arguing, although we hadn't been holding hands. So far, apart from the journey, it had been a pleasant day. Then we came across a fortune teller stall, and as we browsed through her photograph collection hanging outside. Of her stood next to famous people whose fortune she'd told. I wanted to go in and get it all over with. I just needed her to tell me that my marriage isn't over, and it's only a blip. However, I must tell you that prior to getting my fortune told by this lady, I'd only ever had my fortune told once before. It was by a man back in my wild days before I was married. He told me that I would marry a woman with the initial J and warned me that it better not be his wife. That man thanks me to this day, for doing a good job of raising his son Tony.

We both agreed that we'd give this one a go, but Jane insisted that I was to go in first. Which I did, then once I'd closed the door behind me, and sat down opposite the lady, with only the crystal ball between us. I wasn't happy with the fortune she told. 'Jane did love me, but my marriage was over'. My world had just fallen away, I didn't believe her. She then asked who the other lady was. There wasn't one, so I told her so. She then said that I mustn't have met her yet, but when I do it will be tough at first, but don't give up, because she's my special one. She then said to me that I'd had a hard life`, and if I were to write a book about it, nobody would believe it. Amongst other things she also said that she could see me making a lot of money from something that starts off as a hobby, but I'm going to be turn out to be good at it.

As soon as she'd finished I paid her for both mine and Jane's reading, before swopping places with Jane as Hope quizzed me with what she'd said. I told her everything apart from the marriage being over, she was desperate to have her Dad back at home and be part of a family again, as was I. So I told her everything would be OK. As I did to Jane when she returned, before asking what she'd said to her. However, to this day, I still don't know what she did. For the next couple of months things were much the same between Jane and me, I was still desperate to prove the fortune teller wrong and save my marriage. So it was decided that we'd book an August family holiday in the Lake District. However, prior to this Tony had been struggling living alone in his flat, so it was agreed that him and I would get a place together, so I could keep a watchful eye over him. Luckily, we found one which was only seven doors down from Jane's. I also had some more good news prior to our holiday, I'd got a new job. It was thirty-two hours a week, better paid, and something which I was good at. Buying cars from the public.

So life was on the up again, or so it seemed. Me and Tony had settled in nicely, and I'd taken to my new job. The best bit about it though, was that with it being based in an office 35 miles away, I always left at the same time Hope was walking to the bus stop for school, so I'd get to see her daily, and more importantly, Jane and I were still speaking. Until the holiday that was. We had a good time don't get me wrong, but it just wasn't the same. I think we both knew at this point that we'd simply fallen out of proper love with each other. Even though we still cared deeply about each other. So here I found myself still deep with depression, heavily in debt, having just realised that my life has changed forever. I was devastated when I returned home from the Lakes. So I did what I always did, buried my head in work. My job wasn't a hard one. I used to sit behind a desk all day chatting away to private people who were selling their car. The hardest part was figuring out who was telling the truth. So I'd ask them to give me an honest appraisal as I'd buy it anyway, but I'd ask my questions about it in a certain manner, then listen carefully for any hesitations in their reply. I was very good at detecting the liars. Hence, I started to make very good money.

Things were much the same for the rest of the year, I was still seeing Hope most days, Jane was still talking to me. Work was going well, and I'd dipped my toes into the world of internet dating. I didn't stay very long. You see, I'm a talker not a texter, and I'm the sort of person who gets straight to the point. So when I was sending messages asking for a woman's number so we can have a chat, I didn't get any replies. I got bored and gave up. Then Christmas came, the first one where I wouldn't get to wake up and watch Hope open her presents from under the tree. Luckily, Jane was working on Christmas day, so I got to spend the day with Hope at mine, and when Jane came to pick her up after work. She was greeted with a home cooked Christmas dinner. Which she thoroughly enjoyed after her gruelling twelve-hour shift at the hospital. After Christmas things carried on much the same, the only thing which was clearly visible was that Jane and I were drifting apart, each forging our new path in life, which I'll be honest is hard after you've been with someone for over twenty years. Tony had some good news though. He had a steady girlfriend and was moving in with her. Which meant when he moved out at the end of January, I'd have a three-bedroom house all to myself.

February soon came and the day that would change my life forever, only I didn't know it would at the time, it was just the start of my journey as to how I now use writing to control my depression, and believe it or not, it started with a toss of the coin.

Chapter 9

The lowest point of my life.

February 5th, 2019, a day I'll never forget. I was sat at my desk in work viewing an advert for a Mercedes and the pictures were shocking. I was undecided whether I could be bothered calling, so I chose to let the toss a coin decide whether I should. I'd quite often do this in life when I couldn't make my mind up, and I've done it for some big decisions over the years. So to me it was no big thing. Just a bit of fun. Most people call 'Tails never fails', whereas it's heads for me. It has to be the best of three and it must land in my hand. It turned out to be 2-1 to heads so enthusiastically I dialled the number. But I was shocked by the time I'd put the phone down! I've been spoken too sternly in my time, but never as badly as I'd just been, and what made it worse, was that it was by a Lady. However, about an hour later, I got a call from a withheld number. Then when I answered, the lady on the other end asked politely if I was the gentleman who'd called about her car. When I confirmed that I was, in an angelic voice she reeled off the most heart-warming apology for the way which she'd spoken to me earlier. Before explaining how she was recovering from a stroke and my call had startled her from the best sleep which she'd had in ages.

After that we couldn't stop talking, and right from the off this Lady and I opened up about our lives to each other. The car came second, most of the talking was about us two getting to know each other. In fact after we'd been on the phone for over an hour I had to end the call. I could have easily chatted to this Lady all day. However, after work that night. Miranda and I chatted again. For five hours solid, and over the course of the next 48 hours until I had her car collected, we chatted daily on the phone for hours. During our conversations we really opened up to each other and I told her all about my abuse and my wild womanising days before I was married, and she told me about how she'd had tough luck in love, and as a result, was now very suspicious and mistrusting of men. She also happened to be a petite fiery haired redhead, who transpired to be a retired clinical phycologist, and the more Miranda told me about herself, the more desperate I was to help. Then once we'd collected her car on the Friday, this Lady who I'd got to know so well over the past couple of days, was gone out of my life with a simple goodbye text.

Not long after this my Mum was diagnosed with terminal cancer, and we were told that she had six months max to live. Sadly though, with all of her other medical conditions, it would probably be closer to three. Inside I was hurting like never before, but all the while I was putting a brave face on for everyone else. Then when home alone at night I would sit there miserable watching my life rot away. But at the same time, I was quite happy to do so. I'd completely lost my mojo. My mum didn't want to know how long she had left, it was irrelevant to her as she was determined to beat it. As soon as one of my sisters found out she made arrangements for a family gathering in a local park, for the following Saturday. I've got a big family, and It was a joyous occasion, under the circumstances that realistically it would be the last opportunity myself and my sisters would get to be photographed alongside our parents. Nevertheless, we had fun. I made sure of it. I'd brought bats and balls, along with my two super-size water blasters. However, the laughing started before we'd reached the waiting crowd, when as I was pushing my Mum's wheelchair across the grass, she started moaning about it being bumpy. So, I did as I usually did, and being 'Golden balls', I was the only one who could get away with saying it. "Marion. Stop your moaning." Only I jokingly added, "or I'll tip you out of your wheelchair." Just as her front wheel went down a divot, and poor old Marion ended up underneath it on the grass.

The rest of Marion's journey to the waiting gathering went well, and before long she was greeting them all with her usual saying in her best cockney accent. "Hello Darlin. How are ya? I haven't seen you in ages." Shortly afterwards my Dad arrived. One of my other sisters had gone to get him from the nursing home. She pushed him towards my Mum in his wheelchair and positioned it next to hers. Then came a tear-jerking moment. My Dad, who by this time had virtually lost all of his marbles through dementia and was looking very weak and frail. Was sat in his wheelchair, with a big smile on his face, sporting his best flat cap. Then my Mum, who also had a big grin on her face, despite having tubes feeding her oxygen dangling from her nose. Reached out to grab my Dad's hand, and asked him whether he'd been a good boy, before she gave him a big kiss on the lips. Despite all of the confusion racing through my Dad's mind on a daily basis, he recognised instantly who he was kissing, and you could see it by the twinkle in his eyes.

A few days after that Miranda came back into my life and I was happy again. We'd chat for hours when we could, and message when we couldn't. However, our contact developed into an all or nothing pattern. Lots one day, and then silence for days. Nevertheless, we were developing a strong friendship, and I sensed that we were both starting to get feelings. I certainly was. Even though we'd never met. Sadly, Miranda's religious beliefs prevented this from happening until I wasn't a married man. So I set about rectifying the situation, by instructing an online firm to help me in a DIY divorce. As unbeknown to me until I'd called them. Even though we'd only lived apart for a year because I'd slept on the couch for the previous one, that also counted towards the two-year separation. So over the next two months, whilst I was trying to be the strong one to keep my family's spirits up with humour, having Miranda in my life was really helping. I had someone to talk to, who didn't judge me, she just listened and understood because she'd also had a hard life. I was also there for her as she was going through a tough time, and we often talked about why our paths had crossed as we both believe that everything in life happens for a reason.

Then at the beginning of April, my Mum's health deteriorated, and it was now decided that someone needed to be with her twenty-four hours a day. At first my sisters did the majority of the looking after my Mum, whilst I was given the task of visiting my Dad. Daily. Then towards the end of the month, things went swiftly downhill, so I took time off work, and moved in with my Mum 24/7 to look after her and spend whatever time I could with her before she was gone. We had lots of conversations of a night when it was just me and my Mum, but one of my sisters had told me previously, about how my Mum had been telling her how worried she was about me and instructing her to make sure someone looked after me. Then as we were talking one day, she was starting to get confused as her morphine had been increased. And she called me Dave. Instantly, I knew who she was talking about and switched the conversation as I could see the mention of that very man was upsetting her. I did so by telling her to stop crying as she'd start me off, and I was a heartless bastard who didn't cry. I also told her not to worry about anyone looking after me, because I was going to do my job at the head of the family well. But she could feel free to give me a hand from the other side if she could. She replied by telling me that I wasn't a heartless bastard, I was the nicest man in the world, and that if she could help from above, then she would.

Shortly after this, my siblings too took time off work, and together we were determined to respect my Mum's wishes, to die peacefully at home surrounded by her children. Over the next few days, lots of family and friends came to say

57

goodbye to Marion. However, with her fighting spirit, she was determined that she wasn't going to die, and as they left she told them to stop crying before telling them she'd see them all next week, down at the bingo. It was strange the four of us kids sleeping under that same roof after each having gone our separate ways, nearly forty years ago, and when my Mum was resting, we quite often found that the four of us would sit in the dining room, reminiscing our childhood memories.

Miranda and I had been in constant contact throughout this testing period in my life, and looking back on it now, I don't know how I'd have made it through without her. By this time I really believed that she was my special one, I'd developed a feeling inside which I'd never felt before. She was that special to me, that on the Saturday night when all four of us kids were staying over, my sisters had decided that I was to sleep in my old bedroom, forgetting what had happened to me all of those years ago inside it. I didn't want to do it at first, but I was determined that what that man did to me wasn't going to disrupt my Mum's death. That night I finally put closure on my abuse, or so I thought at the time, when I slept in my old bedroom, which still had the same furniture and décor, as it did in the eighties, and I did it by blocking out my nasty memories with nice thoughts about mine and Miranda's future.

Sadly, my Mum died a few days later. But she was at peace now and had got her wish as all four of her children and her were connected by touch, in one way or another. While I said a prayer thanking god for her life, before asking him to take care of her, after she'd taken her final breath. The four of us were distraught, heavily crying and in shock. We all hugged each other in between kissing my Mum's forehead, hoping she'd open her eyes and tell us all to stop 'f in' crying. Then once we'd realised that she'd gone for good, we started informing the family. Over the next two hours lots of tearful people came and departed, before the undertakers arrived to take Marion from her house of nearly fifty years, for the very last time. As the four of us comforted each other while we waved goodbye to our Mum, a white feather blew towards my right shoulder, before touching it and flying off into the distance. That was a sombre moment. We all went our separate ways after that, to start the grieving process in private. Before meeting up the following day to somehow tell our Dad, that his wife had died. However, I had to go and check on him first before I could start grieving. After witnessing my Mum take her final breath only a few hours ago, I now had to go and have a perfectly normal conversation with my Dad who was rotting away with dementia, without bursting into tears, and I didn't know if I could do it.

Luckily, when I got there he was on good form, conducting court, so to speak, with the other residents. So I bought them a coffee and stayed a short while before departing back to mine, and I was just lay on the couch completely numb. Close to breaking point, I was unsure of how much longer I could keep it all together for, but I knew I somehow had to find a way. Luckily for me, I had Miranda in my life. She was very comforting that night, and we spoke for hours on the phone. Then just before bed, and knackered from an emotionally exhausting day, I went outside for a smoke, and once I'd finished, on my way back into the house I paused standing next to the bush in my garden. Before I looked up into the sky and asked my Mum to show me a sign that she was OK. The following morning I awoke late, and as I was brushing my teeth, through the frosted window I noticed what I thought to be a bright purple bed sheet hanging on a washing line. I thought nothing of this until I went downstairs to the kitchen, and I viewed the bush which was green last night when I'd stood next to it and asked My Mum to show me a sign. Only now it was covered in purple bloom. How freaky is that! Soon after this I made my way to the funeral directors to meet with my sisters and make the necessary arrangements to have my Mum cremated. Despite the pain I was feeling inside, I still managed to make everyone smile, by informing everyone before negotiations commenced, that my Mum had worked hard to save for her funeral, so there was no way I was agreeing to anything without us getting a discount. We did get one, a free funeral car. In fact it wasn't as bad an experience as I'd thought it would be. My sisters and I along with the funeral director, frequently laughed throughout our meeting, and that's the way my Mum would have liked it. Sadly, the laughter turned sour with what we had to do next. Tell the sad news to my Dad.

It had been decided that I would go in first to make sure he was ready, as we'd used the excuse that we were taking him for a pint to explain why all four of us were visiting. Then when he was, I'd wheel him outside to the garden, where my sisters would be waiting. He was ready, and he asked me whether I'd seen his mother, knowing full well that he meant his wife. How I kept it together I'll never know, but luckily I did. Then once we were in the garden it was easier with the backup from my sisters. Our Nora did most of the talking. She was the bravest of us all that day. How she had the strength to tell her confused Dad that his wife was dead, without breaking down. I'll never know. But she did it, until she couldn't hold it together anymore, and then someone else would take my Dad's attention whilst she cried with the others, quietly out of his sight. I'll never forget his reaction after he'd just been told that his wife of over fifty years, had died. He sat there confused for a moment, as his brain tried to piece together all of the things that his mind had just absorbed. Then as a tear appeared from the corner of his eye and ran down his cheek, he sounded his reply. "Oh. I'm ever so sorry to hear that. She was a lovely woman." Dementia's a horrible disease, and how I've coped with watching my Dad deteriorate over the years is with humour. Making him laugh every time I saw him, because listening to him laugh and watching him smile, in turn, made me feel happy in an otherwise unbearable situation.

We did take my Dad to the pub for a pint, and we had a bite to eat whilst we were there, and although he thought we were waiting to catch the train, he thoroughly enjoyed himself. Then halfway through the meal, for a moment, his brain had pieced all of the earlier bits of information into his puzzled mind correctly and told us that we'd have to help him make plans for his wife's funeral. This shocked us all, as seconds later his mind had gone again, and he'd just caught the train. We went our separate ways after the pub. My sisters scarpered as they couldn't face leaving him alone in the nursing home. So after I'd taken him back it was off to my house for me. This is the place where over the next few days I rarely ventured out of. Until the Saturday that was. The day of my sisters fiftieth birthday party. She was unsure whether to go ahead with it or not but decided at the last minute that she should. As it's what my Mum would have wanted. I was on Dad duty for the early part of the evening, tasked with the responsibility of getting him there and back to the nursing home safely before I could have a drink. However, everyone had been warned not to mention his wife's death, and to only speak about it if he mentioned it first.

Luckily, he didn't mention it once, he was enjoying himself with food in one hand and a pint in the other, as everyone fussed over him. Once my Dad was safely back in his bed, I was relieved from my Dad duty and after the stressful week which I'd had, it was my time to party. Which I did until four o'clock in the morning. I was the last man standing. However, when I was lying on my couch the following morning I really wished I hadn't partied so hard. I was as rough as a bears backside, and we were due to meet the vicar who was conducting my Mum's funeral at two. I really wasn't looking forward to this, however at just past midday I received a text message that shattered my universe into millions of tiny little pieces.

It was from Miranda, insisting that due to her religious beliefs, for no contact whatsoever until I was a divorced man, and she blocked me from her life. It felt like my body had been ripped wide open and my insides flung out far. I was devastated. She'd been the one good thing which had come out of the previous few months of my life, and now when I needed her most, she was gone. But after having built up such a strong understanding of her, I knew it was a decision which she didn't take lightly, and as painful as it was, I was going to respect it. No matter how long my divorce would take to come through. The meeting with the vicar later wasn't easy, and the four of us were racking our brains as Betty, the Vicar, questioned us over our Mum's life. The meeting lasted about an hour, and for the whole time my mood was getting darker, whilst my mind was questioning how much more I could take before I had a major meltdown. Sadly, it wasn't very long afterwards. In fact it was later that night, about half past ten, when I found myself sitting at the top of my stairs, cooling down after a hot bath, and the only thought that was going through my head was, "I can't take any more. I'm going to end it."

Chapter 10

I'm so glad that I didn't

There I was sat naked at the top of the stairs, looking down at the radiator hanging from the wall at the bottom. Feeling like crap, and without a purpose in life. I'd lost everything. Hope wasn't speaking to me, she was being quite nasty in fact, but I understood why, as she didn't just have to deal with the emotional turmoil of losing her Nan. She was still coming to terms with her family getting ripped apart when Jane and I separated, and because I was always working when she was younger, she blamed me for it. Work was OK, but sadly the man who I was working for had an ego, and I purposely used to wind him up, but get away with it because I made him a lot of money. So, as a result, we never saw eye to eye, and when he flipped, he used his fists. My Dad was wasting away in the nursing home, and it was getting painful watching his daily decline. I was heavily in debt, but at least I was earning a good enough wage to live. The only other person apart from Jane who knew about my depression was Miranda, and now she was gone. She was the one thing in my life which was the ray of sunshine. But that bright light didn't impact the guilt which I was feeling for not being able to make up for all of the lost time in my life, which I never got to spend with my Mum because I was too busy, and took it for granted that she would always be there for me, and now she wasn't, I couldn't take life anymore.

So for the next ten minutes I sat there and worked out exactly how to fall down the stairs and bang my head on the corner of the radiator, with sufficient force and in the right place, that my life would be ended. I was crying uncontrollably when I stood up and placed a towel on the top step, followed by another two steps down. This was so it would look like I tripped on the towels, and as so, it would be recorded as an accident rather than suicide. I stood motionless for about a minute or so, plucking up the courage to do it. Whilst my brain became overloaded with finding a reason why I shouldn't go through with it. Suddenly, a message which Miranda had sent me some weeks earlier raced through it. 'God show's us many path's to choose in life. However, we have to decide which ones right for us.' This was followed by, 'Dead is forever, tomorrow is the first day of the rest of my life.' I sat back down. I was alive, still in a bad way, but thankfully. I was alive. Then later whilst lying in bed I said my nightly prayer, but some weeks earlier I'd added the line, "Please lord show me a way of keeping Miranda in my life forever." So, I repeated this over and over for a while.

Later that night, well it was probably the early hours of the morning if I'm honest, and still heavily shook up. I remembered what the fortune teller in Blackpool had said, about a woman coming into my life, and how it would be tricky at first, but she was my special one. Then I remembered what she also said about if I were to write a book about my life then nobody would believe it. So, as a result, and despite having never read a book in my life, I decided that as a tribute to my late book loving mother. When I got up in the morning, I was going to write a book about the previous three months since Miranda had been in my life. A three months in which a lot of strange things had happened to me, and by doing so it would keep her in my thoughts daily. It would also capture the moment my Mum passed away peacefully at home, but more importantly, it would be written in her name.

It was a bank holiday Monday, about nine in the morning, less than twelve hours since I'd come within seconds of ending it, when I embarked on my mammoth challenge of writing a book. I grabbed hold of my tiny blue laptop as I sat on the couch, before I rested it on my knee. Full of enthusiasm I was determined that for once in my life, I was going to finish something which I'd started. However, my enthusiasm was dented when all I could find to write on was Notepad++. Nevertheless, I opened it, but I couldn't write anything. I didn't know how to start at first. So, I took my mind back to the day I first called Miranda as I thought that would be a good place to begin. I found myself sat on the couch trying my best to recall the events of the day, and before long they came back to me. Not in great detail at first, only key events. I called her; She was very off with me; Called me back apologising; Chatted for ages; Bought car; Chatted again for hours that night. So, I typed these into Notepad++, in real time sequence, but on separate lines, starting with first phone call at the top, ending with chatted again for hours that night. I was made up with myself, I'd made a start. Now all that I had to do was go into a bit more detail, which I did by focusing my mind on the first call, questioning myself, what was I doing, what was I wearing, was it sunny or rainy, who was with me in the office. Etc. etc. I was trying to remember as much as possible, so I could capture it in writing. I found that by breaking it down into key moments and then focusing my memory on each one individually, really helped me remember the detail. I'd also come up with the thought that I'd write it like it was a romantic novel and give Miranda a copy once my divorce had come through, to show her how I'd kept myself busy during her absence from my life and hadn't slipped back to my womanising days. Quite unintentionally I wrote it in third party, past tense.

It was slow going at first but after about an hour I'd come up with, 'My name's Joe, I'm a 48-year-old Single male, who works as a car buyer and one day I phoned a woman up who was horrible to me but phoned back later to apologise.' I laughed reading it back at how pathetic it was, and then I remembered what Alex, my very first sales manager had told me on my first day selling cars. 'Sell don't tell.' Then when I read the sentence again and started to change it, I got scared as my whole upper body and arms became stiff and hard to move. My initial thought was that I was about to have a stroke. This lasted for no more than thirty seconds, but it seemed like a lifetime as you're sitting there, virtually paralysed, wondering what the hell is happening. Luckily, it stopped as quick as it had started. Relieved but unsure what I'd just experienced, I started to think back to the February morning asking myself, "what was I doing?" Then I closed my eyes and could picture everything exactly, just like It was happening now. I could see myself having a bit of light-hearted banter with Tom, while Tony came out of his office with words of wisdom followed by Gill's visit to the photocopier. So I started to write exactly that but in a way as if I were selling it to you, by going into as much detail as I could.

'It was a cold grey miserable February morning, Joe's day started much the same as any other morning, some light office banter with his colleague Tom, a loveable rogue but a very slippery one. Tony, his boss, had come out of his office on several occasions with his 'Look at me I'm so great' ego, for no reason whatsoever but to look down over his workforce, who in his mind, were peasants far inferior to him, checking to see why they didn't have their phones in their hands, cold calling private people selling their cars on Auto trader'.

I couldn't believe it; I'd written a whole paragraph and it made sense without using any big words or swearing. I was well chuffed with myself and for the next hour, my memory, along with my sales skills and limited writing ability, had written another 500 words before my mind went totally blank and the writing ground to a halt. I felt good once I'd finished writing for the day, but more importantly, instead of lying on the couch worrying about how much turmoil my life was in, my mind was firmly fixated on remembering as much from the last three months as I could, so I could convert it to content for my Mum's book, and over the course of the next two weeks whilst I was off work until after the funeral, I spent every spare minute that I could recalling my memories whilst thinking what happened next, good or bad, before I wrote them down in my Mum's book.

What I was getting out and writing bit by bit was helping to ease the pain, and I was finding that whenever I came to a difficult part in my story, and I didn't feel like wanting to write it. What I did instead was to spend the time wisely and re read up to that point, whilst my thoughts were fixated firmly on remembering what came next. Then when the time was right for it to come out, it did easily so I wrote it down before moving on. During this time, I also noticed that my mood was improving. I had a purpose in life, and that purpose was to make my Mum an author. I also found that once I'd written about a difficult part of my life, it didn't cause me pain anymore, just like I'd put closure on it.

Ten days into my challenge, I was flying, I'd done about four chapters and felt good about it. I'd even downloaded something which was better to write with than Notepad++. But sadly, today was the day of my Mum's funeral. So definitely no writing. Today was a day of keeping it together as best as I could, trying to stay strong for my family. I also had the important duty of upsetting the mourners with my tribute speech. I wasn't looking forward to it. My sisters had pressganged me into doing one. 500 words it was supposed to be but had turned into 950. Then once we'd witnessed her take the final curtain, it would be time to get drunk. Very drunk. However, before I set off to meet the rest of my family at the funeral home, I had one last rollie, and once I'd finished it as I threw the stub into my plastic plant pot ashtray in the garden, I looked up into the sky, and asked my Mum to show me a sign that she was OK.

We were all on tender hooks whilst sat in the limousine for the journey to the crematorium. My Dad was in the car with my three sisters and I. He was sat in the row just behind the driver, flanked by Nora and Rachael, which left Tina and me sat at the back. We'd agreed between us that if he asked anything he was getting told the truth. Even though it would crack us all up in doing so. Luckily, he didn't mention it once, in fact, he thought he was going to a wedding. Poor bugger. When we pulled up outside the chapel to be greeted by the crowds who'd gathered, all of them tearful and sad. It was hard keeping it all together. My sisters had lost it, they'd been brave for so long and had reached their breaking point. Then came the moment where I too came very close to reaching mine, just after I'd placed my Dad in his wheelchair, and I witnessed him smiling whilst waving to the whaling crowd.

Luckily, I didn't, and from that point on I regained my strength and humour the best I could, good enough to not only get a round of applause before I'd started my speech, but a standing ovation once I'd finished. Giving that speech is one of the proudest moments of my life. But what came next pulled on the heartstrings of everybody present, when my Dad, aided by myself, stood up out of his wheelchair to place a red rose upon my Mum's coffin. He steadied his body by resting his left hand on the lid, then as he placed his rose upon it, he said the words "goodnight." Before he put a smile on everyone's face, when he waved to everyone while he was getting wheeled out. Saying bye in the way only he could. "Byyyyyyeee."

Once the funeral was over, the partying commenced, and everybody was under strict instructions not to party hard until my Dad had gone. He had to leave and head back to the nursing home for his insulin and tea at four. So for the first two hours everybody was still sober whilst talking, and somehow we got onto the conversation about the book which I was writing as a tribute. Then not very long after, what I'd written so far was getting passed around on my phone for people to comment, and most of them were saying they enjoyed reading it. This put a big smile on my face, even though I knew that they were probably only saying it as not to upset me at my Mum's funeral, but hey-ho, it boosted my determination to make my Mum an author. Then once my Dad had departed the hard partying commenced. I was well and truly mixing my drinks, and I'm not a big drinker. I started off on the lager, then I'd have a vodka with it, the next with a Zambooker, and by the time the venue closed at 8 o'clock, I was legless, but still in the mood for partying. So I went out for a night with my nephew and niece. I don't remember much about it, the first thing I do, is waking up in my Mum's bed the following morning, in my old bedroom, and the thought of what happened to me in it all of those years ago, never crossed my mind once. But a freaky thing happened when I got home to mine. I noticed that the plastic plant pot which I'd thrown my fag end in the as I asked my Mum to show me a sign that she was OK, just before I'd left to cremate her. Had been on fire. But it had only contained damp soil and a dead plant surrounded by the hundreds of other roll ends which I'd previously deposited in it.

It was back to work the following Monday, so my intense writing spell was over, but my determination to succeed was growing stronger. I was really starting to believe that I could really make my Mum an author, and I found myself getting into a pattern whereby I'd dedicate a set time daily as writing time. Incidentally, mine was 7 till 9 at night and as much as I could at the weekends. But the first thing that I would do before writing, was to read what I'd written the previous day, and then when I reached the end of what I had, because during the day I'd been thinking of what came next in my book, the writing just flowed. Then every night before bed, I'd read over what I'd written that night, and I found that the following day, instead of my brain worrying about my miserable life, I was automatically thinking as to what to write next in my Mum's book. Then over time my brain was heeling and the things that were bothering me only weeks earlier, weren't causing me so much pain.

They do say that time's a good healer. It was also keeping Miranda well and truly in my thoughts and I couldn't wait until my divorce came through.

Over the next six weeks, I'd managed to stick well to my writing routine, and I'd finished. 94000 words in that time. I couldn't believe it. I'd found it hard going at times, but luckily for me I'd gained a couple of followers who'd been test readers for me, and every time they said they enjoyed it; I got the leg up I needed to succeed. They also commented on how well I'd hid my depression, and how strange it was to find out by reading it in a book. That was it, I was out. I'd confessed in a book, and something which I'd previously found so hard to talk about, just got a whole lot easier. But more importantly, it was a massive weight lifted from my shoulder. I didn't have to be ashamed to admit that I had problems up top anymore, I could finally talk to people about it, and when you do, you'd be surprised at how many other people are desperate for an ear too.

It was now towards the end of June, and I'd finished my Mum's book, and having achieved what I'd set out to do, to make my Mum an author, gave me a great sense of pride. Also what I'd learnt from the process is that it helped me get through her grieving quicker, and by the time I had finished it, my painful crying was over. I found myself lost and bored again though, and there was no sign of my divorce coming through, so I didn't know how long it would be until Miranda came back in my life. I didn't have anything else positive in my life to look forward to. Then I started to get into my old pattern of vegetating on the couch watching the same old repeats on the telly, and what I found was that as I was lying there, the problems up top which hadn't bothered me whilst I'd been writing, had started to again. My mood was darkening, but luckily I decided to write another book, the sequel to the first, only this one was to be based on fact for the opening few chapters, then the rest would be fiction.

So, for the sequel I soon got into the habit of my writing routine, and it only took a couple of days before all of the horrible depressing thoughts in my head, had been switched to the content of the sequel. I had no intention of publishing the first book as it was written very openly and honest, so I continued in that fashion with this one. Then after only a couple of weeks, and with no sign of my depression resurfacing, my writing stopped when I received a letter from the divorce court, which made me ecstatic. It contained a date for my divorce on it, and it was just over two weeks away. I couldn't write, I was too excited. The hope of having Miranda back in my life, and after not once giving up on believing it would happen, along with my writing, had seen me through.

Chapter 11

It's not quite the end of the long way down yet

My body tingled with joy once I'd received the news, and I immediately sent Miranda an email saying that I'd got a divorce date, and in two weeks' time I'd be back in contact. I also told her that if things had changed for her, and she didn't want me back in her life then all she had to do was send a blank reply, and I wouldn't. I can't overstate how excited I was. That this woman who I'd never met before but had built up such a strong bond and trust for, would soon be back in my life. Writing was out of the window and it was full romantic daydreaming mode for me. I pictured the look in her eyes when we finally met and I handed her a copy of the book, along with a bunch of red roses. My daydreaming mode didn't last very long, as within 48 hours Miranda sent me a text, saying losing me had been like losing a best friend, and that seeing as my divorce was only a couple of weeks away, we could resume contact now if I wanted. Then within minutes I listened to the sound of her angelic voice, as we chatted away right through the night. It was lovely having Miranda back in my life and deciding when and where to have our first meeting was nearing its final stages.

Then Miranda's life which had been flowing along smoothly without me in it, started to have a lot of bad luck in it. I felt guilty from the thought that I could possibly be the cause of it. What with me still being a married man. But I didn't say anything to Miranda, and then one Sunday in July, when things were very stressful in her life, for the first time ever, we ended a phone call with a disagreement. I called her back the following day, but she didn't answer or return my missed call. I didn't try again, just in case me still being a married man was indeed bringing bad luck to her life. I too had a lot on my plate, my divorce would be through by the end of the week, and I was moving back into my childhood home soon after.

You see, back in May all of our family were uncomfortable with my Mum and Dad's house being unoccupied, as it still contained all of their possessions. We were powerless to do anything with them, or the house, because everything had been left to my Dad, and we didn't have power of attorney over him. So until we applied for custodianship, we were snookered. However, one of the conditions of the lifetime mortgage that they took out on it, to bail me out all those years ago. Was that the house must remain unoccupied whilst it was being sold. So back in May, I'd called the creditor and asked them whether I could move in as a guardian of the property, I explained that I was an executor and beneficiary of the will, and was just as keen as them for it to be sold, but I wanted to make sure nothing happened to my parents possessions as, even though they were insured, the memories which they'd help create were priceless. As a result, a lot of them would be getting passed down the family. They verbally said it would be OK, so I asked them to back this up in writing.

Sadly, they must have forget, as did I. Then a few weeks before I was due to move back to my childhood home, I chased up the written confirmation of their permission to do so. They denied all knowledge of my initial conversion, so I insisted that they check their recorded calls. Then only a few days before I was due to move back to my parents and having spent the past few months gearing myself up for leaving the comfort of being only seven doors away from Hope, to the potential nightmare of living back at my parents' house, full time. Alone. I got a phone call from a lady manager at the mortgage company to tell me that she'd checked the recorded calls from the phone numbers which I'd called them from, and not one confirmed that I was told it was OK to move in. I asked what numbers she'd checked my call's from, when she repeated it back to me I realised they'd only checked my work number, so I asked her whether she'd checked my mobile. She hadn't, therefore it was agreed that she would and get back to me as soon as she had. I was fuming. I'd given my notice on the house I was renting. The landlord had already put it up for sale, and someone had put an offer in. My credit rating was bad beyond belief, so I'd never pass a credit check through a letting agency. I honestly didn't know how I was going to cope. The only place I could temporarily move to for a few nights max, was on our Tina's couch.

Over the next few days I drastically searched to find somewhere to rent where you didn't have to pass a credit check. It was hopeless, but just in case I couldn't find anywhere, during this time I'd taken the precaution of moving all of the furniture which Tony had left me when he moved out, into my Dad's room at my childhood home. At least I had my divorce to look forward to though, and on the day it was due to come through, even though we hadn't spoken for days. I decided to send Miranda some flowers for the first time. I called a florist local to her and arranged for a large bouquet of scented lilies to be delivered to her that day. When they asked what I'd like on the card, I told them to write, 'it's official' on one side, and 'you're stunningly beautiful on the other'. After I'd finished ordering the flowers, I called the divorce hotline to see what time mine was due in court. However, to my shock and horror, I discovered that my divorce wasn't final that day, it was only my nisi day. I had another six weeks to wait. My heart fell to the floor upon hearing this, and I got myself quite worked up, having just sent Miranda flowers whilst still being a married man, and I wasn't happy about it. I decided that I wouldn't call, I'd wait for her to call me, and then I could explain my mistake and ask her whether she wanted to cease contact again until the correct date. I waited, and waited and waited, and by the time my moving out day had arrived, she still hadn't called.

Then an hour before I was due to spend the night on our Tina's couch, I received a call from the lady at the lifetime mortgage company, she said that they'd rechecked their recordings and could confirm that they had given me verbal permission to move in, so as a result, I could do so if I still wanted to. After all of the emotional strain caused by the uncertainty, I didn't know if I was up to the challenge of moving back home. So I didn't make any hasty decisions, and I headed for a night on our Tina's couch. But by the time morning came and I'd been kept awake most of the night by her several cats exploring by body lay flat on their couch, my mind was made up that it was Mum and Dad's for me.

I was fretful when I pulled up outside, every time I'd been since my Mum had died there it had never seemed the same. It appeared cold and unhomely, a different feeling than the one which I used to get. However, I remember once I'd opened the door and I entered this time, it didn't seem cold and miserable, it felt welcoming and magical as equipped with just my laptop, I headed straight for the attic. Luckily, during the uncertainty leading up to my move I knew that I'd be in for a testing time up top, and I was fearful as to whether I could stay mentally strong whilst living alone under that roof. So, whilst waiting for Miranda's call, instead of lying on the couch like a cabbage, letting all of the worry and stress send my mental state spiralling. I'd come up with the idea of writing another book to keep my mind occupied. Only this one was going to be purely fiction, and again it would be in my Mum's name. But this time I was going to make her a published author.

Now during my time of telling everyone how I was writing a romantic novel with my first book. Lots of people laughed and said that it would be more like fifty shades of grey, as I didn't have an ounce of romance in me. Therefore, I'd come up with the idea of writing a rude book which would take on fifty shades. So without delay I sat in the attic, where I still had horrific childhood memories from, and didn't write at first, I just smoked away, whilst gathering my thoughts, as I progressed the story in my head. Within a couple of hours I'd come up with a plot.

It was to be about a man who was rubbish at buying gifts for his wife, and when he bought her pans as a present for a previous Christmas, he spent two days unconscious after she'd battered him with them. It's now her upcoming fiftieth and he dreams of giving her something special which she'll remember for the rest of her life. So he asks for a clue. However, when he gets her reply, "Surprise me and use your imagination," his choice of gifts lead him to get on the wrong side of a sadistic sexual cult, and he has to do what no one has ever done before and beat their version of the wheel of fortune game to live. But if he does, he'll walk away with sixty-four million dollars in prize money.

Now over the next four weeks, I found that I was using the same methods as I'd used previously when writing my first book. Set time every day, read what I'd wrote the previous day before writing, and read what I'd just wrote before I went to bed. What I found was that instead of my mind reliving my childhood memories or recalling my Mum's sad death downstairs. It was automatically focussing on progressing my books plot. Even during my normal working day when I was outside from under that roof. I had so much fun and laughter whilst coming up with the bizarre mad plot with all of its twists and turns in it. But as it happens, I found out that I couldn't write a sex scene to save my life. So I use a lot of innuendo's instead and leave a lot to your imagination. Here's an example. 'Bill must have been playing a sad tune on Sandy's organ, because she was weeping, and the more vigorously he played, the harder she wept'. Nothing rude with that sentence. Is there. Then by the time I'd finished writing it, it's 78000 words by the way, all of my horrific childhood memories didn't bother me in the slightest, and I was living a normal happy life under that roof.

However, during the four-week period it took me to complete the first draft, and because I've never read a book in my life, I needed people who would read it and give me their honest opinion as to whether they enjoyed it. It was mainly family members at first, but then I started to recruit customers whose car I'd bought from them. With it being a rude book, I had to choose them carefully. Then once I had, I'd send them over the first three chapters for feedback. Amazingly, it was mostly good. They said the spelling and grammar needed sorting, but the plot was gripping and easy to follow. However, what they really liked was that it didn't contain any big fancy words that they couldn't understand. I was like a dog with two dicks at this point. Loads of people had said they'd enjoyed it. I can't tell you the sense of achievement their comments gave me, and it's words of encouragement like that gave me the strength to carry on with my, what had become a dream, of making my Mum a published author.

Now as it happens, I'd also stumbled across a writers convention on the first weekend of September, and on it, you got two ten-minute interviews with literary agents. These are God's to every aspiring author, as these are the people who can land you a book deal. However, it was £500, and seeing as I'd be booking late, all of the agents representing my genre were fully booked. I'll be honest I wasn't going for the classroom workshops, if I were going to go, I'd only be going for the experts opinion. Undecided, I did what I always do, and tossed a coin. It was 2-0 to heads, so I booked my place, and my literary agent, who just happened to be a middle-aged lady who specialised in children's books, but luckily for me, her agency was now seeking submissions for adult fiction. For my second slot, I decided for a bit of fun, that I would book a fellow author and showcase my Mum's first book to see what she thought.

Now during the time living in my childhood home, and despite what I'd been through since I took the decision to speak out about my abuse, and my current circumstances. For the first time in ages I was enjoying life, and my depression was that much under control. I saw it as when I ran away to join the Royal Navy at the age of sixteen, I was a messed-up teenager. Then when my childhood home was sold and I walked out of the front door for the very last time, I'd be doing so as a mature 49-year-old man. So if I could learn from all of my past mistakes and experiences in life, then I'd be one of the luckiest men alive because I would be getting a second chance in life. As such, I now felt unstoppable. Life was fun again, and even though I had nothing, I was in control of my mental health, and when you are, the feeling is awesome. So, by the time the writers convention came about, and due to the continued good feedback I was getting, I was on cloud nine and really looking forward to it.

However, they weren't ready for me, and my fate was sealed right from the welcome meeting, when one of the panel of literary agents asked if anybody had any questions. Stood at the back, I immediately raised my right arm and luckily for me I was picked. So I blatantly told him, I've got the next fifty shades of grey, would you like it. The room fell silent as everyone glared at me, and from that moment on I was the outcast, but I made sure I had fun. I did get the agents email and sent him my first three chapters along with my synopsis. He replied saying it was a good plot, but my standard of writing wasn't quite good enough. So sadly, he wouldn't represent me.

I was undeterred, I still had my big meeting to look forward to, and before long I found myself nervously sat by a square college table, on an uncomfortable wooden chair, waiting for the expert to come and give me her verdict. I will never forget the look of puzzlement upon the agents face when she told me that I hadn't created a book. I'd created either a blockbuster movie, or a commercial flop. The reason being, there is no book, play, movie, TV series or anything else which has been created to gauge how the public will react to it. She said that if it had been written by a famous person then it would be massive. Her advice to me was to self-publish and test the water. Saddened by the thought that my work wasn't good enough to get a publishing deal, I spent the next six weeks editing my book, before towards the end of October 2019, I took the agents advice, and my dream came true when I self-published on Amazon. What a sense of achievement that gave me. To think I'd actually done it, and my late Mum would be remembered forever for being the author of a book that anyone, anywhere in the world could buy, and hopefully enjoy it.

However, I was now bored again, I'd accomplished what I'd set out to do, and I wasn't in the mood for writing, then one night when I was having a smoke I chuckled as I recalled the look on the agents face when she gave me her comments, and I remembered her remarks about it being a blockbuster film, or a commercial flop. Also as it happens, nearly everybody who'd read the book had said that it would make a brilliant film. It was at that point that I decided to see if I could make my Mum famous by having the words, 'Based on the book by J M Ricketts' in the opening credits of a movie. So I set about opening my Mum a Facebook and LinkedIn account to assist me in landing a deal, and I would search through the movie producers to see who they worked for. I'd then google the company to find their website and give them a call to see if they wanted to make the movie. Sadly, none of them would take a look without a written screenplay. So that was the end of my dream. But I wasn't disappointed or sad, I'd set out to do what I achieved, and I was proud of it.

Now whilst I'd been living the dream of making my Mum famous, my personal life was starting to spiral. Miranda and I had spoken again, on the day of my divorce I sent her a text, asking what happened as one minute she was a big part of my life, then the next she was gone. Then after about a week of communication she was gone out of my life again. The sad thing is, I found out that as I was sat waiting for her to call me, she was waiting for me to call her, afraid to as most of the time previously in her life that someone had sent her flowers, they'd been up to no good, and I was too scared to call whilst still being a married man. The mad thing is, if I had have called Miranda then I wouldn't be writing this book now or have written any of the other three. I'd have only written the first one, because if I had have picked up the phone, We'd have never bloody well got off it. We did used to chat for hours on end, I think our record was seven hours one weekend, and the weird thing is, there was never a moment of silence as we always found something to say.

Work wasn't going well either, two of my colleagues had left during the year after falling foul of my bosses temper, and as such, I knew I was next in the firing line when he blew. The problem was. He uses his fists. Now I'm not a violent man, but if someone attacks me, I'll defend myself until either them or myself aren't moving, and I didn't want that to happen. So I decided that my writing would have to suffer while I went back on the wagons, and within an hour of leaving one job, I was reporting for duty at my new one. It was to be on a 4-on 4-off shift pattern, working nights and sleeping in the wagon during the day. However, it didn't last long, less than ten minutes in fact, when they invited me to take a drugs and alcohol test, and I told them that I'd fail.

So here I found myself with a history of severe depression travelling back home to a house which had horrible memories for me, where I lived alone, and I was now jobless. But on my way driving home I still had a smile on my face, to me this was just another one of life's challenges, and it didn't bother me, because I was in control of my mental health. I also believe everything in life happens for a reason. So that job wasn't meant to be for me. Luckily, within two hours of getting home, I'd gained employment with another company less than ten minutes' drive away from my house. It was less hours and £5000 a year more. But more importantly, I'd be home every night. Incidentally, it was the first job that popped up on the internet. Then after working there for only a couple of weeks, I had a major wobble, followed by another, and they were both at work.

The first one was when I was waiting on the quayside to be loaded, and I witnessed some rowers, rowing in the dock, and the coxswain was shouting his orders. It immediately brought back the memories of when David used to pay attention to me as a child in the Sea Cadets boathouse, whilst people where rowing outside. I then gazed to my left to view the open space which was created when it had to be demolished some years earlier. That sent a shiver down my spine, but it felt like a weight had been lifted from my shoulders.

The second wobble came a few weeks later, again at work, but at the other end of the docks. I was waiting to get loaded with some steel, and throughout the time I'd worked for this company whenever I was loading in this particular area, I'd always find my attention being drawn to the toilets which were situated at the end of the warehouse, next to the quayside. An elderly boatman pulled up to secure an incoming ship, so I got out to have a natter, and we began talking about how busy the docks would have been in it's heyday. He then recalled how the last time he'd seen the docks really busy was when the tall ships visited in 1984. The penny dropped with me after what he'd said. I was there that day, and so was David, and we were alone in those toilets. After I'd had a big wobble it felt like another weight had been lifted off my shoulders, and these events sent me into a period of deep thinking. Sadly, I damaged poor Lulu my wagon that day.

The strange events at work must have hit a chord with me, because I strongly believe that everything in life happens for a reason, so whilst I wasn't writing, I found myself spending all of my thinking time looking at my past life while questioning, what the reason was that something had happened in my life and what did I gain from it. Over the coming weeks I'd worked out that throughout my life, whenever things were tough mentally. I'd cope by sinking my teeth into a new challenge, but sadly when I didn't succeed, I'd feel low, so after another while I'd try something else. Take the time my marriage broke down back in 2014. I used taking on a big boy as something to sink my teeth in, to take my mind of the severe pain my mental health was going through. I also realised that this was the 'all or nothing' pattern that the councillor pointed out to me.

So, I started looking at the circumstances in which I'd conducted my writing. Then I made a connection and I've come up with the conclusion that when my brain is in pain, it knows that I need something to take the agony away, and that's why I try something to distract my mind from it, a new challenge to sink my teeth into. Then when my enthusiasm towards my new challenge disappears because I'm no good at it, it's not because of that at all. It's because I don't need to put as much effort in as my brain has healed over time. Therefore I don't need the distraction of the challenge to take my mind off the pain anymore. So instead of feeling low because I've failed, I think positive because the distraction did what it was supposed to do, help take the pain away, as a result once the pain has gone, it's redundant. If you look at the time I wrote my Mum's second book in the attic, that was the distraction which I needed to keep my mind busy and get me mentally through, but because it was such a painful time, I didn't give up until I'd succeeded. Then once I had, my pain was gone, and I could lead a perfectly normal life with my mental health intact. Then I looked at my Mum's first book and I realised that writing the book was the distraction that I needed to keep my mind busy until Miranda was back in my life, whilst I put closure on my Mum's passing at the same time. This was the moment that I decided to test out my new theory and see if I could use distraction alongside writing to control my mental health, and it wasn't long before I got the chance to put it to the test.

Chapter 12

Getting to know me time

Life had been pretty good up until the middle of December. I was still smiling and feeling positive about things in general. I wasn't living a life of luxury, but I was surviving. My mental health was in good order though as my mind was working on a new book. I hadn't written anything down yet, I was still progressing the plot, but because I was in a happy place, my mind didn't need to spend much time on it. Whenever any bad thoughts came into it I'd substitute them with the plot. Luckily as life was good, I didn't need to speed write this one. Then my life was rocked again, and my mental health questioned, when my Dad was admitted to hospital and we were informed by the doctor's that they didn't think he would make it. I was distraught and already feeling the pressure of this being the first Christmas without my Mum.

I knew that if I was going to be able to cope up top over the coming weeks then I'd need something to distract my mind and keep it occupied. I also thought it only fair that seeing as I'd made my Mum an author, then I should really do something as a tribute to my Dad. However, I didn't have time to write a new book, so that's when I decided to publish the first one as a tribute to him and name it after his boyhood nickname. But seeing as it would also be the first Christmas without my Mum, and I did have a history of buying chocolates from the petrol station on my way over

to see her. I decided that I'd try and give her the best
Christmas present ever, by making her a best-selling
Amazon author on Christmas day. The only problem being
I was skint, so I'd have to do it without spending a penny
on advertising. Luckily, I had a plan.

However, let me tell you how I got on with publishing my
Mum's first book as a tribute to my Dad. Because it was
written using everyone's real names, I had to change these
before I could publish. So I asked people what they'd like
to be called in it. I couldn't believe how much joy and
pleasure they got from knowing that they were going to be
a character in a book. Then once I'd renamed everyone I set
about editing it, but what I found whilst I was doing so, was
that I didn't look at it as being my story, I looked at it as if
it was someone else's and by the end I thought to myself,
what a tough bloke Joe must have been to have survived all
of that. It was only when I came to the happy ending that I
realised it was about me. Then once I'd finished editing it, I
finally manged to put closure on that chapter of my life
when I published it. Prematurely I'm pleased to say, as
thankfully my Dad's still with us. I ordered ten paperback
copies from Amazon to give to family members, but I kept
one for myself, knowing that if ever I was having a bad
day, then a could open the book to remind me who am I,
before I close off that chapter in my life until it's needed
again. I've never once had to open my copy.

So, one distraction down, one to go. Make my Mum a bestselling Amazon author on Christmas day 2019 without spending a penny. Luckily for me, I wasn't looking to make any money from my distraction, so I gave it away on Amazon Kindle for free, and I asked my sister who works at the hospital to download it for me, along with all her colleagues, as well as all of my family and friends. Which they did, and on Christmas day, my Mum peaked as the second bestselling Erotic Thriller Author, in the Amazon free download chart. I can't describe the feeling I felt once I'd achieved this, and this was the moment that I knew I was on to something, and I'd finally be able to use distraction alongside writing to control my depression.

However, the thrill of succeeding, brought out my dream of making my Mum famous again, and early in the new year, I enrolled on a free screenplay writing course. It was bloody tough, I'll tell you and I tried my best, but I struggled. You see, when you write a book it's all about stringing sentences together and capturing the readers imagination. Whereas, with a screenplay it's shorter, straight to the point sentences for both action and dialogue. I gave up trying to write mine after a couple of weeks. Feeling like shit, I went to see my Dad in his nursing home, and during my visit Simon the carer asked me what was up. So I told him I'd quit writing the film. I'll never forget the words he used to inspire me to continue. "Just remember why you're doing it, to make your Mum famous, by having her name light up the screen, every time someone watches it." Thanks Simon.

That was me all revved up and raring to go again, and after watching and reading various videos and blogs, which all said that the first ten pages of your screenplay are crucial in deciding whether your film will be made. I spent the next few weeks writing mine. I did have one slight problem though. I didn't know whether it was any good, and none of my friends could help me. I'd come to an obstacle, now normally in life whenever I'd been faced with something blocking my path, I'd just give up and move onto something else. However, because this was for my Mum, I didn't, and I was sat smoking away one night when the thought of someone who could raced into my mind. A male executive producer, who'd created some easily recognisable TV programmes. He was one of my LinkedIn connections who I'd built up a friendly rapport with after he'd befriended me. Just one slight problem though. He thinks I'm a woman.

Now my Mum taught me that if ever I wanted something in life, then just ask, because they can only say no, but make sure you ask nicely. So I did, and he did say yes, then within a couple of weeks he'd emailed over his recommendations. Things were going great at this point. I was genuinely happy, even though money was tight, but more importantly I was coping with life's everyday up's and down's, whilst my mental health was improving. Then Coronavirus bloody well came along, and all the constant negativity in the news was starting to get me down, I knew I was heading back to the dark days as I'd lost the motivation to write, just when I needed it most.

I was struggling up top, but somehow managing to keep it together. That was until lockdown day arrived.

So here I was back on the slippery slope to depression, sat alone in my childhood home under lockdown, and I knew that before long all of the hard work I'd done to get myself better would be undone. Unless I found something long-term to distract my mind and stop those negative thoughts from returning. Then two days later my sister and I were talking on the phone just after she'd finished a gruelling twelve-hour shift, watching strangers die from this deadly virus, but even though they may have been strangers, she made sure they died with dignity. Her and her colleagues are hero's. They've been on the front line since day one, now exhausted, they are desperate to have something good to look forward to. She was telling me how emotional it was to have exited work on the Thursday to the blue flashing lights and thunderous clapping, but how they were all realistic and they knew that once this virus thing was all over, they'd be treated like the muck on your shoe again.

She also told me how morale was down as they didn't have anything to look forward to. This set me thinking about trying to come up with a national day for the whole nation to use as a distraction to give us all something to look forward to. This would be something that I could well and truly get my teeth into and keep my mind from going crazy. Then after a couple of days I'd come up with something, it was to be called 'Proud to be a decent human day - where everybody's got their part to play'. A day were we paid our respect to the dead, before we applauded each other for playing our parts in keeping each other alive, then we'd hold street parties to rebuild lost communities and firmly cement the foundations of our newfound friendships. Sounds good doesn't it. I went to the press to see if I could get any publicity for it, and they thought it was a great idea, but wouldn't give me any coverage as I was asking for the celebrities and privileged to both organise and pay for it.

Sadly, they didn't think it was worth the exposure as the celebrities would never do it. Even when I explained to them that all I was asking them to do was to publish a story asking a major celebrity the question as to whether they would or not, as I thought that they would say yes, because they were affected with boredom more than anyone during lockdown with their normal lives of glamour and glitz, nowhere to be seen and by far a long way from returning. So I was convinced that they'd welcome something to get stuck in to. However, after sending numerous letters, emails and making phone calls whenever I could, also despite getting to appear on a couple of radio talk-ins, I couldn't find anyone who would give the national day any publicity. Nevertheless this was the one thing which was keeping me from slipping down the slope to the dark days. So under no circumstances, was I giving up until I'd moved out of that house. However, there is a bright side to my efforts, every day the people who knew about it had something else to talk about other than the coronavirus, and just the thought that it might one day happen, brought a smile to their faces because it gave them something to look forward to.

Then, on Wednesday 3rd June things changed drastically, and I now wasn't in control of my life anymore. I'd been sent home from work with the deadly symptoms. I'd had a test, and was back home awaiting my result, whilst my condition was worsening. I didn't know whether I'd get to see Hope or Tony again, or my second chance in life and get to walk out of the front door one last time, or whether I'd be carried out to hospital, breathless on a stretcher. As I'm sure you can appreciate at this point my mental health was tested well beyond it's normal limits, and the pain was bad. However, I chose to write instead to put closure on my lockdown experiences by getting it all out in writing in My Mum's third book. But it also briefly tells people how I used writing to control my mental health just in case I didn't make it.

I did have it, not bad enough to have to go to hospital though. Thank God. Not being able to catch your breath whilst sat down stationary was scary. But after the whole experience by using distraction and writing to control my mental health, I came out the other side mentally stronger. This was me using getting the national day going as the distraction, then when the pain was unbearable, and I couldn't cope anymore, I got it all out by writing. More importantly, I made sure the book had a happy ending.

However, I had to switch all of my efforts to a more pressing engagement once I'd made a recovery. The house sale was going through, and I had to be out in less than four weeks. However, it turned out to be in just over two. I was a bit worried though about finding somewhere to live, what with my credit rating. But luckily Tony still had the phone number of the landlord who he rented his first flat off. So I gave him a call, and by chance he had a suitable one coming up for rent. Then once I'd viewed it, he asked my details so he could perform a credit check. Knowing full well I'd fail I told him so, and then I told him the story about my depression. He rented me the flat without a credit check, and do you know why? He said it was because everyone deserves a second chance and seeing as I was so open an honest with him about my past, he knew that if I was struggling to pay the rent, I'd tell him.

For the last couple of weeks living in my childhood home, it was strange seeing nearly fifty years of memories getting taken down from their resting place, before getting boxed, and taken to its new owner. Then as the house was completely empty I took one final tour, taking time to say goodbye to each room and childhood hiding space, whilst I relived a happy memory. Once my tour hand ended, I opened the front door for the final time, and through it I took the first step into the rest of my life. I'd made it, against all of the odds, and through learning how to control my depression by using distraction and writing, I pulled through, not only with my mental health intact, but I'd also managed to improve it.

Chapter 13

What a feeling

It was great living with the satisfaction of what I'd
achieved up top in such a short space of time, and for the
first time since before I was abused, I had no emotional
baggage. No worries, no horrific memories, and nothing
buried deep which could come back to bite me on the
backside and make me have a wobbly up top. Life was
good, very good. Sadly, it wasn't for some of my fellow
key workers, who were exhausted as they hadn't had any
time off. Luckily though at least we got to have some sense
of normality by going out to work every day. I'll be honest;
it was strange driving my wagon around the deserted roads
of a major city. Then about a month after we'd come out of
lockdown and I was perfectly fine up top, some of my
mates were really struggling, and in need of a real big
boost. So I decided I'd write a book, part fact, part fiction,
and model the characters on my work colleague's and
things which had happened in our daily working lockdown
life.

When I informed them of my intentions, they smiled like a
Cheshire cat at the thought that they were going to be in a
book. Loads of people wanted to be in it, and people were
asking if I could put specific events in it which had really
happened. The atmosphere at work whilst I was writing
was electric, and the staff morale skyrocketed. Everyone
walked around with a smile on their face, and it didn't

matter whether they were in it or not. Just the fact that it was getting written was giving us something other than the Coronavirus to talk about. But the fact that it would be published so the whole world could read about their lockdown experiences, made then feel really special.

Then once I'd finished writing it, I published it on Amazon as a 'Rom-Com'. It is. Only a very rude one if you've got a dirty mind, as it's full of innuendo's, in fact the only rude sentence in it is the first one. "Sorry I'm late Jessie, Anthony had a ****-on and it was a shame to let it go to waste." Once it was available on Amazon I ordered multiple copies and gave each person whose got a character in the book based on themselves a signed copy with a personal message in it, thanking them for being a character in my book. What a talking point when having guests round for dinner they've got for the rest of their lives with that. They've also got something else to look forward to, any profits that are made from book sales are going into a kitty, so that next summer we can all have a day out together in Blackpool. Sadly, it's not looking good as we've only raised £12.83 so Far, but there's still time and the book keeps us talking every day. In fact they're already trying to persuade to me start writing the sequel. So that's how I'll use writing in the future to help raise the spirits of others.

Things had been rosy since I'd published my Mum's fourth book, I know four, I still can't believe it myself. But my life's certainly taken a turn for the best since I took to writing barely 18 months ago. I'm so glad I did. Four books, each written under a completely different mentally testing time, and by writing each one, I've learnt how to be in control of my mind. I've also given up smoking, and cannabis. I don't need that anymore to help me forget.

However, November the 2nd came. Lockdown 2, and although I wasn't trapped in my childhood home this time, as I'm in my new flat. I found myself with a lot of extra thinking time, but the urge to write wasn't there. I'm also now approaching the age of fifty and my mind's started wondering back to the previous decade in my life and recalling what a downward journey I've had. As I look at what I have now in life, compared to my fortieth. Back then I had a loving wife, two kids, friends, a nice house, my own business, and along with it came the money. Now there's just me, divorced, skint, living in a rented flat. All of the friends and possessions are gone, and even though I don't know what the next decade has in store for me, I do know one thing. I'm really looking forward to it, because for the first time in years, I'm in control of my mental health. I'm also going to make up for lost time with Hope.

But I've got to survive lockdown 2 first, so I've decided that I'm going to use the time wisely and whilst I'm sat alone in my flat recalling my life's events from the past decade, instead of letting them get me down and start me on the slippery slope to depression again. I've taken a week off work so I can speed write them down in this book to help me put closure on it. The worst decade of my life. To make sure nothing from it comes back to bite me on the backside and ruin my second chance in life. Also sharing my story with you will help me put closure on the guilt which I have lived with up until this day, that others got hurt and have had to go through the same mental suffering as me, because I failed to speak out when I should have. As with it now being published, it will remain in print forever, so people will be able to read it, and hopefully find using distraction alongside writing to control their mental health, helpful to them.

I hope that my openness and honesty regarding some truly personal details in my life may encourage anyone who has read my story and is suffering in silence to speak out. If you are please talk to someone about it now. Don't be afraid, no one will think any different of you, and if they do, you're better off without them in your life. Don't leave it for so long that it gets as bad as I let it. The hardest part is taking the first step, by reaching out and talking to someone. It's all downhill from there. It may be a long hard battle, but a battle that with help and support you can win. Just never stop believing in yourself that you can do it. Then once you have, you too can appreciate the beautiful feeling which takes up your insides when you're in control of your mental health.

Sadly though, I've forgotten about my earlier confession, the one thing that can come back from my past to haunt me.

Stealing the missing landmarks from This Morning's Weather Map.

Consequently, Richard and Judy, my fate is in your hands. Therefore, if you think that this story is a whole pack of lies, and has been written by some drug taking, criminal, ex car salesman who has a very creative imagination, and he's trying to use it to get him off the hook. Then you have no choice but to find me Guilty, as confessed, and I'll start my second chance in life with a criminal record. Just like I did in my first. However, if you think it's all true, as indeed it is, then it would be a miscarriage of justice if you gave any other verdict than Not Guilty, and help me take one step closer to my dream of making my Mum famous, with the awarding of a coveted Richard and Judy 5-star review!

The End

'Everything in life happens for a reason, to give you the content to write your book'

J M Ricketts

Now for anyone who would like to try and incorporate writing as a way to control their mental health, here's my advice. When using it to put closure on a sad chapter of your life, start your book at a happy period just before it. But, before you even start writing, for the first few days spend all of your spare time wisely by recalling events from that moment on, to give you the initial content for your book. Make sure you're open and honest with yourself and try and recall as much detail as possible. Ask yourself, where was I, how was I feeling, what was I wearing. The more questions you ask yourself, the more content you'll remember for your book. Then pick a happy ending, any ending you want, as long as it involves you being happy.

What you'll find is that after a couple of days your mind will naturally wonder to the content of your book, automatically whenever negative thoughts appear in your head. Then after a few days of thinking, you'll know when it's time to write your book. I can't stress how important having a set routine that you can stick too is. Mine was 7 till 9 PM weekdays, and as much as I could over the weekend. But I appreciate for some that may be far too much. I'd recommend that you do at least thirty minutes a night from Monday to Friday. There's no rush, and some nights you won't feel like writing. Don't worry, it's natural. Just make sure you still use the time wisely and re-read what you've already written, then the following day, use your thoughts to think what happens next. Whatever needs to come out, will come out when it's ready. Then once you've written it down, it will feel like some pressure's been released, and then the rest of the book will flow. What you'll find is that when you're re-reading what you've written the night before you start again, you'll make changes as you are, and as a result, some nights you'll spend all of your writing time repeatedly making minor adjustments to your previous text until it feels right. To me, it was like my brain wouldn't let go until it read right in my book. It's your book, take as long as you want, but the sooner you finish it, the sooner you'll get to your happy ending.

Once you have, re-read the whole book at least three times, again you'll find that you'll make changes. Once you're happy with it, change everyone's name in it, then leave it for a few months while you carry on with your normal life, and you'll feel a sense of achievement now that you're an author. For some of you it make take weeks or even months before you start writing. It doesn't matter. Just try to keep recalling as much detail as possible, and then when the times right, you'll start writing. All you've got to do is teach your brain to automatically switch to the content of your book, every time you get any negative thoughts.

About three months or so after finishing your book, open it once again, this time to edit it. What I found from doing this is that with all of the characters having changed names. I believed I was reading someone else's true story and thought how strong they were to have gone through what they had and survived. Then when I got to my ending, I took strength from realising that it was a story about me. Once you're happy with the edit, self-publish it on Amazon. Order as many copies as you want, and don't worry about other people being able to buy it, list it in some obscure category like, learning math's, and just put a small description like, 'A book about hippos', also age rate it 18+. Then the chances of someone who's looking for a maths book and deciding to buy yours are very slim, and once your copies have been dispatched, simply withdraw it from sale. Give copies to your closest friends, after reading it you'll be amazed how much they've learnt about the real you. But more importantly, keep one for yourself, then if ever you're having a bad day, you can pick it up and have a read. To remind you how strong a person you are, before you close over your book on that chapter in your life, until you need to take strength from it again.

What I also found helped was having someone read over what I was writing as I was going along. Chapter by chapter, and just having someone there to talk to about it during the writing, really supported me a lot. Don't worry about the spelling or grammar either. It's your story, in your words. How it's wrote doesn't matter, what does, is that it sounds right to you. That's all that counts. Anyway there's plenty of free writing software available for downloading to help you with this.

Now a good way of keeping negative thoughts at bay, whilst you're waiting to conduct your edit, or just for life in general, is to write a fiction book. Believe me it's fun, especially if, for writing purposes only, you name the main character after yourself. All I do prior to writing is use all of my thinking time wisely to come up with a rough plot, along with a suitable start and ending. I don't worry about the rest; I know I'll make it up as I go along. Then once I've got one, I'll write and I'll follow the same writing, reading, and thinking routine as I did for closure. The only difference being instead of my mind recalling real life events, I was letting my imagination have fun. Thus cancelling out any negative thoughts. However, once writing had commenced, and my imagination ran wild, the ending which I had planned initially, was nowhere to be seen. Let your mates read it as you're writing along, and if they think it's any good once it's finished, then why not publish it. You never know, it only takes one person to read it and like it to change your life, and people love reading a gripping story. Just make sure you rename yourself before you publish. Again it doesn't matter how long it takes to write, just use your plot to substitute any negative thoughts.

If the pains really bad like it was when I was isolated under lockdown, and I struggled to write, that's when to use a physical distraction. A new hobby or challenge in your life. Do this for as long as you can to keep your mind occupied, then when the pain is unbearable like it was for me when I was waiting for my coronavirus test result. It's time to write about what you achieved, and how you did it during that new hobby or challenge. When writing use the same reading, writing, and thinking process as for closure. What you'll find is that you'll spend a lot more time writing when your minds under this much mental strain and it will flow. But again, make sure your book has a happy ending. Then once you've written it in your book, the pain will have subsided, and you won't feel sad in yourself that you've tried something new and failed. Again, you can publish it if you want. You never know.

This one's my favourite. When I'm perfectly fine up top but my work mates are suffering. It was so simple, all I did was ask my mates who wanted to be a character in book, and for one thing that they'd like to do in it. Their answers told me the plot. I just had to use my imagination to make it all fit together for its happy ending. Their mood was instantly lifted, as the talk of the workplace was all about the book. They're still talking about it today some three months on, and they'll always have their own signed copy as a momentum. As well as potentially a day out in Blackpool from any book sales.

Now during these testing times, everyone's mental strength has been tested differently, but we've all been affected in one way or another, so we're all going to need to put closure on this horrendous coronavirus period in our lives. Why not see if you can put closure on your own lockdown memories by writing your very own true story of how, when your life changed for the worse overnight, you manged to stay strong, and somehow managed to pull mentally through.

'Everything in life happens for a reason, to give you the content to write your book'

J M Ricketts

This is a true story and apart from Richard and Judy, all names have been changed to protect the innocent.

If you're alone or a victim and you've got no one to talk to here's some useful numbers of people waiting to help.

The Samaritans 116 123 calls are free from any phone, they won't judge or tell you what to do, they'll just listen.

MIND the mental health charity 0300 123 3393 calls are free

CALM Campaign Against Living Miserably 0800 58 58 58

Victim Support 0845 30 30 900 If you're a victim of rape or sexual assault whether you've reported it to the police or not, they're here to help.

Rape and Abuse line, all calls are handled by women

0808 800 0123

Survivors UK - Male rape and sexual abuse line

0845 122 1201

If you're a victim of child abuse and it's happening now dial 999. If it's historic then dial 101 to report it.

Printed in Great Britain
by Amazon

28561131R00066